Making it and Breaking it

Making It and Breaking It

The Fate of Public Interest Commitment during Law School

Robert V. Stover

Edited with an Introduction by
Howard S. Erlanger

UNIVERSITY OF ILLINOIS PRESS
Urbana and Chicago

Manufactured in the United States of America
C 5 4 3 2 1

This book is printed on acid-free paper.

Library of Congress Cataloging-in-Publication Data

Stover, Robert V., 1944–1986.
Making it and breaking it: the fate of public interest commitment during law school / Robert V. Stover; edited with an introduction by Howard S. Erlanger.
p. cm.
ISBN 0-252-01557-6 (alk, paper)
1. Public interest law–United States. 2. Law students–United States. 3. Professional socialization–United States. 4. Law students–Colorado–Denver. 5. Professional socialization–Colorado–Denver. 6. University of Denver. College of Law.
I. Erlanger, Howard S. II. Title.
KF299.P8S76 1989
340′.023′73–dc19 88-12100
CIP

To Carissa

Contents

Tables

Foreword

One can probably say of almost any book that a great deal about the author is to be discovered between its covers. Anyone who has written a book knows how much heart and soul goes into the effort. Yet there is a tradition in the social sciences of trying to remove oneself from the analysis and interpretation—of achieving the ever-elusive goal of "value-free" social science.

Robert V. Stover did not believe a value-free social science was desirable or possible, as any reader of this volume will immediately recognize. He did not hide his own values. In fact, he wrote the book because of the values he held and in order to effect social change consistent with those ideals. Perhaps the values of an author are always evident, no matter how mightily he or she strives to submerge them. But in this book, one encounters more than Bob's values and preferences about his subject. Parts of the book are autobiographical, drawing upon Bob's experiences and observations as he went through law school with those who were the subjects of his research. Each chapter, for example, begins with a vignette describing some aspect of Bob's experience selected to illustrate an important point of the analysis which follows.

If his values are brought plainly out in the open in this book, Bob certainly is not blind to the need to marshal evidence in support of his argument. Indeed, this book is a rare combination of frankly personal observations and sophisticated statistical analysis of quantitative data. It is a mark of Bob's honesty that he felt compelled to present his own perspective so clearly. It is a mark of his skill as a writer and analyst that he was able to integrate his personal experiences so well with a carefully constructed and executed social scientific design.

The commitment to using the law on behalf of the disadvantaged in society, the recognition that law is a social and political instrument of extraordinary power, and the persistent search for ways to better the human condition through political change were all values at the core of Bob's life. At the time of his death, Bob Stover was a highly respected member of the Department of Political Science at the University of Colorado. His students knew him as a demanding and innovative teacher who was constantly searching for ways to demonstrate the political promise and limits of American law. He had mastered the traditional Socratic method of teaching case law; he was a leader in the department's quantitative methods program; and he frequently demonstrated principles of the law using classroom simulations. To say the least, his students were never bored.

Yet Bob's commitment extended well beyond the classroom. In addition to an active and visible program of research, of which this book is an example, Bob pursued a public interest law practice of his own. Having taken time from his duties in the department to attend law school, Bob immediately began to practice what he preached. For example, through his *pro bono* work for the ACLU, he took a First Amendment case on behalf of an indigent client. He carried out an incredibly thorough investigation (logging many miles and hours), researched the law, assisted in the trial, and won. Bob saw his participation in that case as yet another opportunity to blend his personal experience with his scholarship. He had begun work on a book about the case—and about the politics of federal trial courts—when he became ill. Unfortunately, he had completed only fragments of that manuscript by the time of his death.

As Bob carried out the writing and analysis of the present book, I was privileged to have numerous conversations with him. I have since gone through his files, so I have some idea of whom Bob would have thanked as his book goes to press. I am sure I will fail to mention others, and I trust they will understand nonetheless how much Bob appreciated their help. The data used in this project were collected with the financial assistance of the National Science Foundation and the Committee on Research and Creative Work of the University of Colorado. Neither institution, of course, bears any responsibility for the interpretations offered here. The students at Denver University ("DU") Law School who participated in the study were obviously essential. I know Bob especially appreciated the many hours given by his in-depth respondents who are frequently quoted in these pages, although never identified by name. He wanted to protect their anonymity, but he valued their contributions very highly. Their pseudonyms serve the dual function of hiding their identity and demonstrating their puckish author's boyhood attraction to a certain midwestern major-league team. A number of administrators at DU helped him with the fieldwork by providing him a place to collect his questionnaires, by including his materials in registration packets, and by encouraging registrants to respond to the survey.

Bob greatly appreciated the intellectual and personal support he found in the Colorado Department of Political Science. His leaves to attend law school were supported by the department, and his colleagues and friends there provided him with many opportunities to try out his ideas. He loved to argue and found right at hand many good-natured combatants to engage. The department also provided ample computer time and secretarial assistance. Special thanks should go to Janet Ames for typing and retyping the early drafts of the original manuscript.

Bob would have particularly wanted to acknowledge the meticulous assembly and editing of the final manuscript by Howard Erlanger of the University of Wisconsin. Howard's careful and thorough editing is testimony to his skill as a writer and scholar, as well as his respect for Bob's original ideas and style. Those of us who want to remember Bob by what we read in these pages are most grateful. I wish to thank Larry Malley, editor at the University of Illinois Press, for his faith in this project despite the fact that he and Bob never met or discussed the book.

I have no doubt about the dedication. Bob's relationship to his daughter encapsulated and redefined his life. Theirs is an inspired example of the love and support that can transcend tragic illness and even death.

Bob met his illness and death with grace and humility, even as he fought with all his might to overcome his disease. He once said, "I could ask, Why me? But I also have to ask, Why not me?" That relentless integrity which characterized Bob's life and work is well represented here. The book stands as a fitting memorial to a man who cared.

Walter J. Stone
Associate Professor
Department of Political Science
University of Colorado, Boulder

Acknowledgments

My work as editor was facilitated by a summer mini-grant from the University of Wisconsin Law School, for what was anticipated to be just a month's work. I would like to thank John Kidwell, Walter Stone, and especially Charles Halaby for their helpful comments on the original manuscript, John Manzo for research assistance, and Theresa Dougherty for a yeoman's job in typing the final version and formatting the tables.

Howard S. Erlanger

Introduction

It is always a shock to lose a colleague in the prime of his career, but the death of Bob Stover is especially upsetting because of the substantial work that he had in progress. I am honored to have been asked to bring the main piece of that work to fruition.

My involvement in this project has been akin to that of a midwife. I worked from Bob's drafts of ten chapters and several additional unpublished papers. He had not had time to organize or document his data sets, so as a practical matter it was not possible to verify his findings or carry out any additional analysis. My role was to produce a publishable manuscript, which I did by extensively rewriting and reorganizing the materials to create the six chapters that appear in this volume. The primary casualty of this process was an analysis of job preferences that accounted for aggregate change using a coefficient of aggregate impact. Bob was very much interested in this method and had prepared a paper advocating its use and giving an example based on the data set reported here.[1] However, the analysis was not sufficiently complete to allow inclusion in this volume.[2]

Superficially, this book does not much resemble the drafts I started with. However, while my editing was extensive, I made every effort to remain true to Bob's analysis and to maintain his style and point of view.[3] My goal was to make his presentation more complete and more effective, not to replace it with my own. This is not to say that I have any substantial disagreement with Bob's analysis; overall I found his arguments to be quite convincing. Nonetheless, had he lived, I suspect we would have continued to engage in dialogue about the work; some of my concerns are indicated later in this introduction.

I first met Bob when I served on his dissertation committee in 1972. Shortly after that I began work with Doug Klegon on a panel study of changes in University of Wisconsin law students' orientations to public interest work, and at that time Bob and I began a long and rewarding exchange of views on the subject. Klegon and I eventually published an article arguing that, while the students did become less interested in public interest law, the content of legal education is not the primary source of that change.[4] Following the lead of Becker[5] and others, we concluded that law students are relatively insulated from whatever process of socialization the law school might attempt and that the influence of the job market was probably more important in shaping career choices. In a later article I carried the argument further, using some hypothetical models of the market for public interest jobs.[6]

Bob challenged these assertions by assembling an impressive body of quantitative and qualitative data on students at the University of Denver College of Law. In 1982, Bob published an innovative analysis of the "supply side" of the market for public interest lawyers in the *Law and Society Review*.[7] I had made assertions about students' willingness to take public interest jobs. Bob set out to measure that willingness at various wage levels so that he could estimate supply curves for different law jobs. He concluded that DU students' job preferences changed so much during the three years of law school that the quality—and probably also the quantity—of students available to do public interest work greatly diminished. He argued for increased funding for public interest jobs but especially felt that law schools should "make a comprehensive and systematic effort to impress upon their students the importance of the legal profession's responsibility to provide legal service for all."[8]

In that article and in a companion piece published the same year,[9] Bob acknowledged that the key to his argument was his assertion of a causal link between legal education and changes in job preferences. He wrote: "In the near future I hope to be able to *explain* shifts in supply. I am currently at work on an analysis that attempts to explain the changes in terms of a model that conceptualizes job preferences as a product of *values* (wants, needs, and desires) and *expectations* (perceived probabilities that particular jobs would gratify one's values positively or negatively)."[10] This book represents Bob's development of that explanation.

Much has been written since 1982 on the content of legal education and its effect on student attitudes, professional orientation, and job preference.[11] Law school deans and eminent scholars continue to criticize the narrow focus of legal education,[12] and some in the Critical

Legal Studies movement have held that legal education diverts students interested in leftist politics and instead serves to reproduce a liberal capitalist social order.[13] But many have continued to reject the notion that legal education socializes students to reject public interest work or to embrace corporate practice,[14] and it is safe to say that the debate remains alive today.

Bob's book is based on three sources of data: a panel study, for which 103 DU students completed questionnaires at the beginning and end of their law school careers; frequent interviews with nine students who began law school with a strong commitment to practicing public interest law; and Bob's experience as a DU law student during the data collection period (1977–80).

Bob found that the number of DU students who hoped to work in public interest law declined by half during their law school careers, dropping from one-third of the students at the beginning of law school to one-sixth at the end. He explains this shift by conceptualizing job preferences as the product of values[15] and expectations, arguing that people will prefer those jobs they think will fulfill important values. As a result, people's job preferences change in response to changes in their values and in their expectations about the ability of various jobs to fulfill those values.

Several kinds of changes in values and expectations contributed to the decrease in preference for the four public interest jobs on which Bob focused—work in a public defender office, in a legal services office, in a minority rights organization, and in a public interest law center specializing in environmental and consumer law. There was a decline in the desire to use one's position as an attorney to help others and to work for social and political change; there was a decline in the expectation that public interest jobs would in fact allow a beginning attorney to accomplish those altruistic goals; and there was a reduced expectation that public interest jobs would enhance long-term career prospects by providing a new attorney with valuable experience, knowledge, and contacts. At the same time, increased expectations of craft satisfaction (such as the opportunity to do innovative and creative work, feel the satisfaction of producing results, and challenge one's ability) contributed to an increased preference for conventional business practice—and especially for a job with a large corporate law firm.

The erosion of professional altruism began early, as students directed their attention to coping with the hectic, emotionally draining first year of law school. Bob argued that altruistic values might have reasserted themselves during the second and third years, but the dominant professional culture—as manifested both in the law school and in the conventional law firms where many students worked—largely ignored altruistic concerns. At the same time, the dominant culture emphasized a broad range of competing values. As a result, students not finding refuge in a public interest subculture were not likely to leave law school with their altruistic values intact.

Two sorts of learning processes contributed to changes in students' expectations about various jobs. In part the lay mythology with which students entered law school was replaced by a more accurate experience-based picture of both conventional and public interest practice. For example, students learned that corporate and business practice is not necessarily a tedious, stifling regime but can be challenging and exciting. They also gained a more realistic picture of the limited resources and heavy caseloads that burden many public interest attorneys.

But in addition, Bob inferred that students "overcorrect," setting aside lay mythology only to replace it with a mythology provided by the legal profession. Students who found themselves drifting away from public interest practice allayed their guilt by quickly and uncritically accepting unfavorable images of public interest practice and favorable images of conventional practice. These changes in expectations then tended to strengthen the decline in preference for public interest practice.

Bob concluded that the students who retain altruistic values do so through interaction with others of like mind—in the "public interest subculture." DU students had three potential points of contact with that subculture: the Student Law Office, the student chapter of the National Lawyers Guild, and public interest employers in the Denver area. But only about half of those who started law school with a public interest preference connected with any of these institutions. In part this was because these "public interest centers" did not permit participation by first-year students, while their appeal to second- and third-year students was limited by location, time demands, or narrowness of political ideology.

As far as public interest law is concerned, Bob saw law school as being like a set of bookends without books. Convocation speakers often speak of the professional obligation to help, but the subject is largely ignored day to day—when it might really make a difference. One might argue that the relegation of equal justice concerns to ceremonial occasions reflects the primary method of control in our society by which power is legitimated through the granting of symbolic—rather than genuine—rights. Bob was intrigued by this critical approach, but he believed that many law academics were sympathetic to liberal reform—often having engaged in it themselves—and that the system could be reformed from within. He also did not want to argue that law school is responsible for the problem in some moral sense. Instead, he took a pragmatic approach, arguing that even if the law school is not part of the problem, it is part of the *solution*, because legal education can make a difference and it can be changed. Although he ultimately hoped for more, his immediate aim was to maintain and encourage the public interest concerns already held by a significant minority of law students, by creating a viable public interest subculture that would reduce the isolation these students usually experience.

A major strength of Bob's contribution is his integration of method. His panel questionnaire allowed him to establish that goals, expectations about jobs, and job preferences all change during law school. But quantitative studies of this type generally suffer what might be called the "black box effect." While we know change has occurred, we don't know how or why it happened, and when we find that two characteristics both changed over time, we don't know the causal order of the change. Bob's qualitative data allow him to make reasonable inferences regarding these issues.

While information on the intervening period could have been obtained through quantitative methods, Bob's qualitative data lend a special depth to the analysis of the process of change and add richness and authenticity to the story. Bob was a great raconteur, and few law school graduates will fail to recognize their friends—and even themselves—in his vignettes about the futile quest for the penultimate outline, the search for the after-hours study-nerd, or the incredible difference between life in the first and second years. Of course, Bob is not the first law student to write about his experiences,[16] but his unique contribution is his focus on the *consequences* of the events and processes he describes.

Had Bob survived, I have no doubt that he would have elaborated his model of changes in values, expectations, and job preferences. As the analysis stands now, it is driven by two goals that are somewhat in tension. On the one hand, Bob was deeply concerned about the drift away from public interest law as a job preference, and he wanted to analyze the causes of that change and recommend reforms. This led him to focus on those independent variables—changes in goals and in expectations about jobs—that are most susceptible to intervention. But at the same time, he hoped to develop a more general model of job choice.[17]

Development of such a general model of job choice could well begin with the job preferences of entering students and the identification of the demographic, socioeconomic, and personal variables associated with those preferences.[18] One might then analyze changes in job preference over time, taking these variables into account. Analysis by multivariate techniques[19] would probably produce a complex model that would allow for the assessment of interaction effects and the evaluation of the net effect of changes in values and expectations.[20]

One factor relevant to a general model of job choice is the effect of gender, which Bob was working on at the time of his death.[21] At the end of the third year, women students were three times more likely than men to prefer public interest practice. Just 5 of 53 men (9%), compared to 14 of 50 women (28%), named a public interest job in response to an open-ended question about their preferred initial full-time job.[22] Bob considered three explanations for this difference in job preferences: the possibility of gender differences in professional altruism,[23] perceived alternative employment oportunities[24] or constraints imposed by marriage and parenthood.[25] Of the three, differences in altruism appear to be the most important. Seventy percent of the women, compared to 35% of the men, scored above the overall mean on a scale measuring the importance of opportunities for professional altruism in their first job as an attorney. Women were also somewhat more likely than men to believe that they had better chances of getting a job in the public interest sector than in private practice. However, married women and especially women with children (who are generally believed to prefer the flexibility often provided by public interest jobs) were in fact less likely than single or childless women to prefer public interest jobs.

Bob also examined several path-analytic models, including one that assumed that professional altruism was a consequence of perceptions about employability in the public interest sector, and found again that differences in altruism were the most important determinant of job preference. Unfortunately, this is the only accessible information on the impact of gender; there is no analysis available for the effect of gender on initial job choice or on changes in goals or job preferences. In addition, no inferences about gender can be drawn from the reports of the in-depth interviews, because a comparison of manuscripts indicates that the pseudonyms do not necessarily reflect the gender of the respondents. Thus we cannot say, for example, whether the existence of supporting subcultures is more important for men or for women.

Another area in which Bob was still developing his ideas was the policy recommendations that followed from his analysis. His chapter on policy, the last one he wrote, was an early draft. As a stimulus to further thinking on the subject, some of that material is included here in chapter 6. I am sure Bob would have noted with approval the recent article by Jan Costello, whose perspective is much like his. Like Bob, Costello concedes that most law students are not interested in left-oriented public interest law. Her ultimate focus, therefore, is on those students with some inclination toward altruism; she seeks to "substantially increase the likelihood that a student with the potential for a public interest law career will discover that vocation."[26] Her proposal is designed to "give law students (1) an opportunity to identify with powerless clients, (2) experience in the role of an attorney representing the powerless, (3) a realistic possibility of job placement after law school, and (4) temporary financial assistance to pursue their choice of a public interest career."[27] Bob would also have taken heart in the work of the National Association for Public Interest Law, which now has chapters at over thirty-five law schools. NAPIL chapters raise money by soliciting donations from students (who contribute a percentage of their earnings from conventional summer jobs), from conventional firms recruiting at the law school, and from other sources, such as faculty and alumni. The funds are used to give students subsistence support in public interest placements during the summer. In 1985, NAPIL chapters raised a half-million dollars, which funded 250 fellowships.[28] Finally, he would have been pleased to learn that Tulane University School of Law recently instituted a requirement that students perform *pro bono* work in order to graduate.[29]

One aspect of law school on which Bob did not focus is the admissions process. Yet I believe he would have been receptive to the arguments of those who say that "what goes in, comes out" and that the admissions process is the most important activity at the law school. Monroe Freedman, for example, has written:

> What happened, then, to all those others who entered law school with the sole goal in mind of righting social wrongs? . . . Those people never existed. Law school did not destroy their sense of social justice, because they never had it in the first place. . . . We admit people into law school principally on the basis of their technical skill. . . . We give virtually no weight in the law school admissions process to a candidate's manifest concern with social problems.[30]

Little systematic information exists about the admissions process, but it is clear that historically, at least, some admissions committees have been most interested in developing and maintaining an elite status for the bar.[31] Today there is probably little outright discrimination, but many factors, including the tendency of many schools to rely heavily on the LSAT and undergraduate grades, serve to shape both the characteristics of the student body and, perhaps as important, the characteristics of those who apply for admission.[32]

Finally, there is the issue that formed the impetus for this project—the question of the relative importance of the job market as compared to what happens in the law school. I think that Bob has convincingly made the case that what happens during law school is important, even if it is not determinative. The obligation to engage in public interest work is important enough, and the need for expansion is great enough, that the problem should be addressed on multiple fronts.

I believe that Bob's book, while not definitive, is one of a handful of essential works on the socialization of law students. Other books about student life have been written by law students, but they are based on anecdotal data. Other panel studies have been done by scholars, but none has made extensive use of both quantitative and qualitative data. Other critiques have been made, but few have been as measured or as well grounded in empirical data. Bob's book stands alone as an in-depth analysis of process and outcome in legal education, using a full breadth of data sources and addressing a scholarly issue with important policy implications. To paraphrase Edward Corbin's comment, when he completed a task similar to mine: In times like these, it is comforting to realize that length of life is not essential to completeness of living. Short as his life was, Bob Stover lived successfully.[33]

NOTES

1. Robert V. Stover, "The Coefficient of Aggregate Impact: A Method of Accounting for Aggregate Change," *Social Science Journal* 24 (1987): 127–38. Posthumous publication arrangements were handled by Walter Stone.
2. In addition, one reviewer questioned whether this method was the best way to approach the analysis of Bob's panel data. Because the data were not accessible for reanalysis in any case, the matter was never resolved.
3. The vignettes are his, as are the references to my work.
4. Howard S. Erlanger and Douglas A. Klegon, "Socialization Effects of Professional School: The Law School Experiences and Student Orientations to Public Interest Concerns," *Law and Society Review* 13 (1978): 11–35.

5. Howard S. Becker, Blanche Geer, Everett C. Hughes, and Anselm L. Strauss, *Boys in White: Student Culture in Medical School*, (Chicago: University of Chicago Press, 1961).
6. Howard S. Erlanger, "Young Lawyers and Work in the Public Interest,"*American Bar Foundation Research Journal* 1978 (1978): 83–104.
7. Robert V. Stover, "The Importance of Economic Supply in Determining the Size and Quality of the Public Interest Bar," *Law and Society Review* 16 (1981–82): 455–80.
8. Ibid., 478.
9. Robert V. Stover, "Law School and Professional Responsibility: The Impact of Legal Education on Public Interest Practice," *Judicature* 66 (1982): 194–206.
10. Stover, *Law and Society Review*, 457 n. 2 (emphasis added). Bob believed, however, that even if the changes in job preferences or in concomitant attitudes and expectations resulted from forces outside the law school, legal educators still would have an obligation to do whatever possible to stem the tide. See his *Judicature* article at p. 206.
11. For summaries of work prior to 1982, see the articles by Stover and by Erlanger and Klegon (cited above), as well as the annotated bibliography by Kenneth H. Berry and Patricia A. Connelly, "Research on Law Students: An Annotated Bibliography," *American Bar Foundation Research Journal* 1978 (1978): 751–801, and Thomas L. Shaffer and Robert S. Redmount, *Lawyers, Law Students, and People*, (Colorado Springs: Shepard's/McGraw-Hill, 1977).
12. Derek C. Bok, "A Flawed System of Law Practice and Training," *Journal of Legal Education* 33 (1983): 570–85. See also David Riesman, "The Law School: Critical Scholarship versus Professional Education," *Journal of Legal Education* 32 (1982): 110–19, and Harold Berman, "The Crisis of Legal Education in America," *Boston College Law Review* 26 (1985): 347–52.
13. The significant recent works include Duncan Kennedy, "Legal Education and the Reproduction of Hierarchy," *Journal of Legal Education* 32 (1982): 591–615; James C. Foster, "The 'Cooling Out' of Law Students: Facilitating Market Cooptation of Future Lawyers," in Richard A. L. Gambetta, Marlynn L. May, and James C. Foster, eds., *Governing Through Courts*, (Beverly Hills, Cal.: Sage, 1981), pp. 177–90; James C. Foster, "Legal Education and the Production of Lawyers to (Re)Produce Liberal Capitalism," *Legal Studies Forum* 9 (1985): 179–211; and Robert Granfield, "Legal Education as Corporate Ideology," *Sociological Forum* 1 (1986): 514–23.
14. The major recent work here appears to be that of Audrey James Schwartz,"The Paper Chase Myth: Law Students in the 1970's," *Sociological Perspectives* 29 (1985): 87–100, and James M. Hedegard, "Causes of Career-Relevant Interest Changes Among First Year

Students: Some Research Data," *American Bar Foundation Research Journal* 1982 (1982): 787–867. See also the earlier work of these authors: Audrey James Schwartz, "Law, Lawyers, and Law School: Perspectives from the First-Year Class," *Journal of Legal Education* 30 (1979): 437–69, and James M. Hedegard, "The Impact of Legal Education: An In-Depth Examination of Career-Relevant Interests, Attitudes, and Personality Traits Among First-Year Law Students," *American Bar Foundation Research Journal* 1979 (1979): 791–868.

15. To many scholars, the term "values" connotes something more deeply held, fundamental, and group-based than the phenomenon Bob was measuring, and I considered changing Bob's term to one with less intellectual baggage, like "goals." I retained Bob's term because I think that he would have been concerned that just as "values" connotes something deeper than he measured, "goals" would connote something more trivial and ephemeral. Bob was concerned with value change among law students as a fundamental process, not merely as a change in preferences. Nonetheless, although this question is conceptually and empirically important, I do not think it is central to the persuasiveness of the argument in the book.
16. See J. Osborne, *The Paper Chase*, (Boston: Houghton Mifflin Co., 1971), and Scott Turow, *One L*, (New York: Putnam, 1977).
17. One consequence of the approach Bob took was that even when he did analysis at the individual level, his decision making was influenced by his interest in explaining aggregate change. For example, in the stepwise regression analysis for table 2.7, he rejected variables for which aggregate change was not significant at the .15 level. As a result, if a potential independent variable had a large effect on changes in job preferences, but the individual changes in that variable cancelled each other out, that variable was inappropriately eliminated from further consideration.
18. Job preferences are likely to be affected by many factors besides the goals and expectations Bob emphasized. These factors include race, gender, age, religion, parents' work, marital status, family responsibilities, anticipated debt at graduation, and anticipated academic performance. Many of these variables have been found to be predictors of the type of job held by graduates, although there has been dispute over whether the distribution primarily represents choices made by the attorneys or by their employers. See John P. Heinz and Edward O. Laumann, *Chicago Lawyers: The Social Structure of the Bar*, (New York: Russell Sage Foundation; Chicago: American Bar Foundation, 1982); Howard S. Erlanger, "Lawyers and Neighborhood Legal Services: Social Background and the Impetus for Reform," *Law and Society Review* 12 (1978): 253–74; Cynthia Fuchs Epstein, *Women in Law*, (New York: Basic Books, 1981); Geraldine R. Segal, *Blacks in the Law: Philadelphia and the Nation*, (Philadelphia: University of Pennsylvania Press, 1983); and the works cited in

Erlanger, "The Allocation of Status Within Occupations: The Case of the Legal Profession," *Social Forces* 58 (1980): 882–903.

19. One might also measure variables through the use of indices, rather than the single-item indicators Bob used. One consequence of using many individual items in an exploratory regression analysis, as Bob did, is that on probabilistic grounds alone, some will be significant. In addition, when many variables are entered simultaneously in a regression model, the chance of explaining a significant amount of variance is increased. Therefore, to some extent Bob's method biased the findings toward the conclusion that changes in values and expectations were more important than the competing explanations evaluated in chapter 5.
20. It might also entail an in-depth look at the people who "switched the other way," for example, the two people who preferred a public interest job at the end of the third year but who did not express that preference when they entered law school.
21. The following material is based primarily on Bob's unpublished paper, "Gender Differences and Desire for Public Interest Practice Among Law Students."
22. The broad definition of public interest job, discussed in chapter 2, was used. The difference reported in the text is statistically significant at the .01 level.
23. See, for example, Carol Gilligan, *In a Different Voice: Psychological Theory and Women's Development*, (Cambridge, Mass.: Harvard University Press, 1982), especially chapters 3 and 4, and James C. Foster, "Antigones in the Bar: Women Lawyers as Reluctant Adversaries," *Legal Studies Forum* 10 (1986): 287–313.
24. See, for example, Eve Spangler, Ronald M. Pipkin, and Marsha Gordon, "Portia Faces Life: Sex Differences in the Professional Orientations and Career Aspirations of Law Students" (Paper presented at the annual meeting of the American Sociological Association, Chicago, 1977).
25. See, for example, "Project: Law Firms and Lawyers with Children: An Empirical Analysis of Family/Work Conflict," *Stanford Law Review* 34 (1982): 1263–1308.
26. Jan C. Costello, "Training Lawyers for the Powerless: What Law Schools Should Do to Develop Public Interest Lawyers," *Nova Law Journal* 10 (1986): 438.
27. Ibid. at 438–39. Costello, like Bob, believes that the decision to take a job in the public interest sector is significantly influenced by exposure to alternatives to the conventional professional orientations: "Most law students . . . will only have the opportunity to identify with powerful clients—and with those who serve them. Although law students come from a variety of social and economic backgrounds, the vast majority are from middle class or upper-middle class backgrounds, either from educated families or with a strong 'white collar'

identification. Before law school they probably have had very little contact with powerless people. If they are not encouraged to pursue that contact during law school, it is not surprising that they will choose to work for a client group with whom they are more familiar, more comfortable—with whom they share a common identity'' (438). A similar theme is noted by Granfield (''Legal Education as Corporate Ideology,'' cited earlier). In my own work, I concluded that identification with the interests of underrepresented clients was one of several factors that explained why persons who took their first job in the public interest sector were very likely to continue their involvement. Howard S. Erlanger, ''Social Reform Organizations and the Subsequent Careers of Participants: A Follow-Up Study of Early Participants in the OEO Legal Services Program,'' *American Sociological Review* 42 (1977): 233–48.

For information about jobs in the public interest sector, see Geoffrey Kaiser and Barbara Mule, *The Public Interest Handbook*, (West Cornwall, Conn.: Locust Hill Press, 1986).

28. Edward A. Adams, ''Nation's Students Tax Themselves to Fund Public Interest Fellowships,'' *National Law Journal*, July 6, 1986, p. 4.
29. ''Pro Bono at Tulane,'' *American Bar Association Journal*, December 1, 1987, p. 34; Edward A. Adams, ''Tulane Students Must Undertake Pro Bono Work Before Graduation,'' *National Law Journal*, March 14, 1988, p. 4.
30. Monroe H. Freedman, ''The Loss of Idealism—By Whom? and When?'' *New York University Law Review* 53 (1978): 658.
31. See especially Robert B. Stevens, *Law School: Legal Education in America from the 1850s to the 1980s*, (Chapel Hill: University of North Carolina Press, 1983).
32. See Howard S. Erlanger, ''Toward a Sociology of Law School Admissions,'' *J. Legal Education* 34 (1984): 374-84.
33. Edward S. Corbin, Foreword in Benjamin R. Twiss, *Lawyers and the Constitution*, (Princeton: Princeton University Press, 1942).

1 Bookends without Books
Law Schools and the Obligation of Public Interest Practice

Law School and Altruistic Ideals

Dozens of other entering law students and I rose in a standing ovation for the fiery young public defender who admonished us to "just once" think about the poor and dispossessed persons we would inevitably abandon. "You *will* sell out to those with money and power!" he thundered. "But before you do, *just once* consider and understand the needs of those without the resources needed for adequate legal counsel in the United States today."

The time was September, 1977; the place, the University of Denver College of Law; the occasion, one in a series of orientation sessions for beginning law students. For two days we had listened intently as a succession of professors, lawyers, judges, and students alternately soothed and fired our fears of the years ahead. We had been welcomed and warned, pitied and prodded, admonished and applauded. The law school, the legal profession, and our own abilities and aspirations had been the objects of endless acclaim. The program was impressive, especially the remarks by members of the faculty. One professor after another revealed the secrets to success in law school with rare wit and intelligence.

But no speaker that week moved us like Larry Pozner, the public defender who dared us to meet his high ideals by proclaiming anyone's plans for practice in the public interest to be pipe dreams and mockingly predicting surrender to service on behalf of the privileged classes. Perhaps our enthusiastic applause revealed a high commitment to those ideals, and our individual certainty that while others might bend, we would not. Or perhaps it signified no more than incipient boredom with the message of the earlier speakers and our appreciation of Pozner's fiery oratory and tell-it-like-it-is style.

Probably it was some of each. Questionnaire data I gathered during the early weeks of that first quarter of law school identified a solid minority of students who aspired to public interest practice and many others who were interested in the area. When asked to designate the single job from a list of twenty that they would consider most desirable as an initial full-time job after graduation from law school, 33% of those responding chose a public interest job. And as reported in more detail below, when they rated all twenty jobs, three public interest jobs ranked among the top five.

A little more than three years later, in October, 1980, many of us who had cheered Larry Pozner's speech again sat together in a large auditorium listening to another round of exhortations to live up to our professional obligation to public interest practice. The occasion was our induction to the bar of the State of Colorado. The speaker was Justice Jean Dubofsky of the Colorado Supreme Court. The tone of her speech was less strident, but the moral conviction behind it was no less fervent than that we had witnessed three years before. "According to the Code of Professional Responsibility," Justice Dubofsky emphasized, "persons unable to pay should be able to obtain necessary legal services and lawyers should support and participate in that objective. . . . If you don't begin to contribute . . . now, it will be difficult later. . . . Please take seriously the fact that with your license goes the obligation to contribute your skills as lawyers to and for the public good."

The polite, almost strained applause that greeted the end of Justice Dubofsky's speech stood in stark contrast to the spontaneous ovation that had marked our enthusiasm three years before. As I glanced at the faces around me, I thought I saw lowered eyes, guilty half-grins, almost imperceptible shrugs of indifference, and even a few disdainful smirks. But perhaps I was so caught up in the irony of the situation that I only imagined these reactions. In my mind I saw bookends, neatly spaced, but without books. For in the years since Larry Pozner's speech, I had heard hardly a word of the lawyer's professional obligation to public interest practice.

One day at the beginning of my first quarter in law school, our contracts professor devoted a few minutes to the lawyer's obligation to "tithe of his talents," describing his own *pro bono* service. Over the next couple of months, that professor made occasional passing references to the importance of public service. During my three years of law school, there was little other mention of public interest law during class. One professor described his efforts on behalf of needy tenants, and a couple of others made brief passing references to their own activity in the public interest, but in most classes the subject was completely ignored. In my class on the legal profession we proceeded section by section through much of the Code of Professional Responsibility, focusing on a multitude of ethical and professional dilemmas a lawyer might face, without once squarely addressing the Code's admonition "to participate in service to the disadvantaged." The school's basic litigation program—in which interested students received credit for representing indigents facing minor criminal charges —was "sold" to students primarily as a way of getting practical experience rather than as an opportunity to fulfill one's professional obligation of *pro bono* practice.

Near the end of my third year, service to the disadvantaged was lauded to a few top students at the induction ceremony for the Order of St. Ives, an academic honor society. But this was the exception that proved the rule: the call to public interest practice was reserved for ceremonies marking beginnings or significant achievements; it was not an item for everyday consumption. When symbolic intonation of high professional calling was in order, the ritual chant of public service was again repeated to help secure the myth of privilege with responsibility. The rest of the time it was ignored.

There is no reason to suspect that DU is atypical in this regard. If anything, it is probably more concerned than most law schools with producing responsible and compassionate professionals. It offers the opportunity for students actually to engage in public interest practice through a clinical program that provides academic credit for a wide range of practical experience, much of it oriented toward serving the economically disadvantaged. And the DU faculty includes a significant number of persons whose careers show a genuine commitment to social justice. But evidence of this commitment to serving the underrepresented was virtually absent in the classroom.

My research shows that my classmates' desire to practice public interest law decreased significantly during the course of their legal education. For example, the 33% who in the fall of 1977 chose a public interest job (from my list of twenty) as most preferable for an initial full-time job shrank by half during the law school years. And the number of public interest jobs rated among the top five on the list fell from three to one. Data from other law schools are consistent with this pattern.[1]

It would be foolish to attribute this change solely or even primarily to the law schools' failure to emphasize the lawyer's professional obligation to serve the disadvantaged. The reasons for the decline include many factors, both internal and external to law schools, and a primary purpose of this book is to provide some insight into how these factors operate. But even if the movement away from public interest law could be shown to result entirely from external forces, the law schools might succeed in creating countervailing internal forces, if they tried. If the legal profession has a collective obligation to provide adequate legal representation for all, it seems reasonable to ask the law schools to act affirmatively to attempt to ensure that their graduates begin their careers with an enthusiasm for public interest practice equal to the enthusiasm they had when they began their law school careers. After describing and attempting to explain law students' declining desire for public interest practice, I will suggest some steps which legal educators might take.

Concepts and Methods of the DU Study

For purposes of this study, "public interest practice" refers to legal representation of individuals and interests who would lack adequate representation if they had to rely exclusively on their own resources.[2] Examples of these individuals and interests include poor people, many persons and groups with civil rights and civil liberties claims, and many environmental and consumer groups. At the time I began my research, most public interest litigation involved working for goals more congruent with the philosophy of the political left than with that of the political right, in large part because the left has been far more sympathetic to the reformist goal of aiding marginal groups and interests. Since that time, a number of "conservative public interest law firms" have sprung up whose stated aims include serving the underrepresented.[3] However, because my questionnaire was written prior to this new development, my data focus on liberal public interest practice.

Public interest law is often practiced on a full-time basis by lawyers employed by public defender offices, legal aid offices, public interest law firms, and the like; alternatively, it may be practiced on a part-time basis by attorneys taking certain cases on a low-fee or no-fee basis (*pro bono* practice). This study focuses primarily on the full-time practice of public interest law.

In explaining the decline in students' desire to practice public interest law, I view changes in job preferences as a product of changes in the person's *values* and changes in the *expectation* that holding a who observed or participated in certain events at DU during the period of the study. This information was included in the book only after receiving permission from each person whose identity might be revealed. No students other than the nine listed, and no faculty, are referred to by name, either real or fictitious. Occasional references to others by name (such as those earlier in this chapter) refer to their actual names.

The students I formally interviewed and the others who responded to my written questionnaire knew that my research was focused on job preferences, but they did not know that I was particularly interested in public interest practice.

An Overview of the Book

Chapter 2 reviews the quantitative data on changes in job preferences, personal values, and expectations about the characteristics of different law jobs. In it I argue that a significant factor in the changed job preferences is a change in values and expectations. Chapters 3 and 4 use the interview data to take an in-depth look at the process by which these changes come about. In chapter 3, I look at changes in students' values, focusing on the types of changes that occur in the first and subsequent years in response to law school and community experiences. In chapter 4, I analyze changes in expectations about the characteristics of different law jobs and consider some of the sources of these changes. In chapter 5, I examine several alternatives to my focus on values and expectations as key factors in changing job preferences, including "aging," shifts in political orientation, and changed perceptions about the market for public interest lawyers. In chapter 6, I analyze the importance of subcultural support for the maintenance of public interest commitment by law students, and I close with some recommendations for reform.

NOTES

1. These data are cited in chapter 2.
2. For a useful conceptual discussion of public interest law, see Burton A. Weisbrod, "Conceptual Perspective on the Public Interest: An Economic Analysis," in Burton A. Weisbrod, Joel F. Handler, and Neil K. Komesar, eds., *Public Interest Law: An Economic and Institutional Analysis* (Berkeley: University of California Press, 1978), pp. 4–29.
3. Karen O'Connor and Lee Epstein, "Rebalancing the Scales of

Justice: An Assessment of Public Interest Law," *Harvard Journal of Law and Public Policy* 7 (1984): 483–505.

4. James C. Foster, "Law as Liminal: Becoming Lawyers in America" (Paper presented at the annual meeting of the Law and Society Association, June 1983, Denver), p. 9.
5. The data on LSAT scores, undergraduate grade point average, and prior residence are from a law school fact sheet compiled for both day- and night-division students. The data on prior residence may be slightly misleading in that some students who had resided in Colorado for some time before entering law school were nevertheless listed as being from states of earlier residence.
6. Because the students completed their legal studies at varying rates, not all of my subjects graduated in May, 1980. I administered the second questionnaire to graduating subjects every quarter from fall, 1979, through fall, 1980. The 11 persons completing the questionnaire in fall, 1980, included 8 who did not graduate that quarter, either because they were pursuing joint degree programs or because they had shifted to part-time programs. These 8 persons are included with the 103 respondents on which my analysis is based.
7. When asked to "describe the form of employment which ideally you would like to have for your initial full-time job after graduation," 24 women and 14 men gave answers that expressed at least an ambiguous preference for public interest practice. When asked to rate the desirability of each of twenty jobs on a ten-point scale, the 50 female respondents gave a total of 110 eight-point, nine-point, and ten-point ratings to the seven public interest jobs on the list, whereas the 53 male respondents gave a total of only 80 such top ratings to those jobs.

2 Singing the Blues
Erosion of Public Interest Preferences

It was finals week of the first quarter. I sat in the library, my feet propped up on the table, a well-used spiral notebook in my hands, memorizing the law of property. I'd been there all day, and my level of restlessness increased with each arcane rule of law that my mind absorbed. As the afternoon passed, the frequency of my trips to the water fountain and restroom increased geometrically. Around four o'clock, I once again pushed back my chair, stood up, and walked out of the library into the hall. Moving as slowly as possible, I bypassed the second-floor men's room and descended the stairs.

As I pushed open the door to the first-floor restroom, I was greeted by a blues melody. Inside one of the stalls, someone was playing the harmonica and singing, "I got the law school blues, ya dooba, wabba, doo—and I bet you got 'em too." A buoyant feeling of relief swept over me as I laughed for the first time that day. Someone's creative impulse, humor, and sense of proportionality had survived finals week! By the second verse, I recognized the voice. It was Nelson Fixx, a fellow first-year student, one of the nine with whom I was conducting in-depth interviews for my research.

I told Nelson later that listening to him sing the blues in the men's room was the high point of the first quarter of law school for me. Nelson himself was one of the high points of our class in my opinion. Before starting law school, he'd taught kindergarten, worked as a carpenter, sold automobiles, and spent four years with a social service agency organizing the inner-city poor. He was a conscientious objector during the Vietnam War and had participated actively in the presidential campaigns of liberals George McGovern and Fred Harris. During our first quarter of law school, he organized an effort to get every first-year student to sign a sympathy card for a professor whose wife had died. He was continually collecting contributions from friends to buy birthday presents for other friends. He wore big floppy hats to parties and had a dog named Cassidy that sang when Nelson played the harmonica.

Nelson started law school planning to practice public interest law. In answering my first questionnaire, he described the job he'd most like upon graduating as employment by "an environmental planning commission for a region of Colorado—preferably a small free-wheeling team making legislative recommendations." A liberal, pro-environmental orientation was evident from his answers to other questions as well. The job from a list of twenty (see table 2.1) that he marked as most preferable was "attorney for a 'public interest lobby group' for which you did litigation, lobbying, investigative research, political organizing, and public relations." His second choice was "attorney for a non-profit 'public interest' law center that specializes in environmental and consumer law."

When I interviewed Nelson at the end of the first quarter, he told me, "I want to be able to work at something that I can feel good about on the weekends at home, so I feel that I'm using what I know in some constructive way for the greater good—if there is such a thing. . . . I don't want to work for corporate interests. . . . I don't want to work for interests that I see have given us the pollution and the Disneylands of the world—the more and more plastic that will last beyond us as many generations as we can see into the future."

But even then, in his typically honest and introspective fashion, Nelson expressed doubts about that vision. He openly volunteered the possibility that he might change his career aspirations, noting that age seems to make people more conservative and that legal education seems to corrode what once had been clear-cut moral certainties. "Sometimes, I wonder," he said. "The more law school I have, the more I wonder."

By the time he graduated, Nelson had changed his vision of the ideal first job and was seeking employment as a deputy district attorney or as a clerk for a federal judge. After passing the bar exam, he took a prestigious position as a clerk for a judge on the U.S. Court of Appeals.

Nelson's initial desire to practice public interest law was shared by Betsie Pierce. Betsie was active in the women's movement before entering law school. She majored in women's studies and later taught a course on Women and Mental Health at her undergraduate institution. As a participant in a state women's conference, she helped draft

Table 2.1 Job Descriptions in the Questionnaire

Public Interest Jobs

Staff attorney for the American Civil Liberties Union

Attorney for a legal aid or legal services office, handling civil cases for poor persons

Attorney for an organization working to protect the rights of a racial minority group, such as the Native American Rights Fund or the NAACP

Attorney for a public defender office, handling criminal cases for indigent defendants

Attorney for a non-profit "public interest" law center that specializes in environmental and consumer law

Attorney for a "public interest lobby group" for which you did litigation, lobbying, investigative research, political organizing, and public relations

Attorney for a small law firm (2–6 attorneys) that does a *large* amount of free "public interest" law in addition to normal income-producing work

Attorney for a federal agency in the social services area, such as Health, Education, and Welfare or Housing and Urban Development[a]

Other Government Jobs

Deputy district attorney, prosecuting criminal cases

Attorney for a federal regulatory agency, such as the Securities and Exchange Commission or the Interstate Commerce Commission

Attorney for a typical state or local governmental agency

Clerk for a state supreme court justice

Business-Oriented Private Firms

Attorney for a large law firm (20 or more attorneys) that specializes in corporate law

Attorney for a medium-sized law firm (10–16 attorneys) that specializes in business and corporate law

Attorney for a small law firm (2–6 attorneys) that specializes in business law

House counsel for large or medium-sized corporation[a]

Other Private Firms

Attorney for a medium-sized law firm (10–16 attorneys) with a general civil practice

Attorney for a small law firm (2–6 attorneys) that specializes in criminal and personal injury litigation

Attorney for a small law firm (2–6 attorneys) with a general civil practice

Working for yourself as a solo practitioner, attempting to build a practice from whatever cases are available[a]

[a] Related to but not specifically included in this category.

a set of demands forwarded to the National Women's Conference in Houston in 1976.

In response to my first questionnaire, she described the job she'd most like upon graduating from law school as "work in a legal clinic specifically oriented toward the needs of female clients." The job she designated as most preferable from my list of twenty was "attorney for a legal aid or legal services office, handling civil cases for poor persons." During her first year of law school, Betsie was awarded a grant that allowed her to spend the following summer counseling battered women and drafting a pamphlet on their legal rights.

Betsie made top grades throughout law school. By the time she graduated, she probably could have found employment with a prestigious law firm, but her concerns lay elsewhere. Although her interest in women's law diminished somewhat during her law school years, her desire for public interest practice remained constant. In responding to my questionnaire in her final quarter of law school, she wrote, "Although I am not yet sure what my ideal job would be, I believe that I would most like to work in a poverty law clinic in the metropolitan area." Her top two choices from the list of twenty were "attorney for a legal aid or legal services office, handling civil cases for poor persons" and "attorney for a public defender office, handling criminal cases for indigent defendants." A short time after answering my questionnaire, she accepted a job with a public defender office in Denver.

The varying paths taken by Nelson and Betsie are representative of those students in my study who began their law school careers aspiring to public interest practice. Some, like Nelson, changed direction and ultimately sought employment in other areas of law. Others, like Betsie, remained steady in their commitment to serving the under-represented. Overall, there was considerable erosion in desire for public interest practice. This chapter will describe the extent of this erosion, and will show the relationship of the shift in job preferences[1] to changes in the students' values and their expectations about the characteristics of particular jobs.

Changes in Job Preferences During Law School

My written questionnaire used two approaches to measure students' desire for public interest practice. First, an open-ended question asked the students to "describe the form of employment which *ideally* you would most like to have for your *initial full-time job after graduation*." Depending upon the stringency of the criteria employed, the number of students whose answers expressed a desire for public interest practice at the beginning of law school was either 29 or 38 of the 103 panel respondents.[2] During the law school years, these numbers were about cut in half—reduced from 29 to 15 using the stringent criteria and from 38 to 19 using the lenient criteria. The shifts in preference were almost entirely in one direction. Of the 38 students expressing at least an ambiguous desire for public interest practice during the first quarter of law school, 21 shifted away from public interest practice. But of the students initially not expressing such a preference for public interest practice, only 2 shifted toward public interest law during their law school career.[3]

The second method of measuring the students' desire for public interest practice used the twenty job descriptions listed in table 2.1. As shown by the grouping of these jobs in the table, I considered seven of them to be public interest jobs. (An eighth—working as an attorney for a federal agency in the social services area, such as HEW or HUD—arguably could be added to the list.) The questionnaire asked the students to circle the job from the list of twenty that they would consider most preferable for their first full-time job after graduation. During their first quarter of law school, 33% of those responding chose one of the seven public interest jobs; but by their final quarter of law school, only 16%[4] chose one of the seven jobs.[5]

The questionnaire also asked students to rate each of the twenty jobs on a ten-point scale in terms of desirability as a first job after graduation (table 2.2). At the beginning of the students' law school careers, three of the five most popular jobs were in public interest practice, and three of the five least popular jobs were with business-oriented private firms. By the students' final quarter of law school, only one public interest job was among the five most popular. On the other hand, "attorney for a medium-sized law firm that specializes in business and corporate law" advanced from sixteenth to third in the ratings. And "attorney for a large firm that specializes in corporate law" moved from twentieth position to tenth. The mean ratings fell over time for all of the public interest jobs and rose for almost all the jobs with private law firms. All the business-oriented jobs showed an increase over time.[6]

Table 2.3 reports the percent of respondents at both points in time who rated each job highly, scoring it eight or higher on the ten-point scale. Looking at the data in this way allows us to check for the possibility that the drop in mean ratings for public interest jobs was caused primarily by downward shifts among persons who even initially did not care much for such jobs.[7] We can reject this possibility because the number of high ratings dropped for every public interest job on the list (see table 2.3). This drop was sharpest for jobs with a public

Table 2.2 Job Preferences of DU Students

	Time 1 Mean Rating	Time 2 Mean Rating	Mean Change in Rating
Public interest jobs			
ACLU staff attorney	5.56 (8)[a]	4.69 (14)	−.87**
Legal aid or services	5.65 (7)	4.89 (11)	−.76**
Minority rights organization	5.32 (11)	4.24 (17)	−1.08**
Public defender	5.28 (12.5)	4.76 (12.5)	−.52*
Public interest law center	6.15 (4)	5.19 (9)	−.96**
Public interest lobby	6.46 (2)	5.38 (6)	−1.08**
Small firm—much public interest work	5.80 (5)	5.55 (5)	−.25
Mean for category	5.75	4.96	−.79**
Federal social service agency	5.45 (9.5)	4.27 (16)	−1.18**
Other government jobs			
District attorney	5.17 (14)	4.23 (18)	−.94**
Federal regulatory agency	5.45 (9.5)	4.76 (12.5)	−.69**
State or local agency	5.13 (15)	4.19 (19)	−.94**
State supreme court clerk	6.53 (1)	5.64 (4)	−.89**
Mean for category	5.57	4.70	−.87**
Business-oriented private firms			
Large firm, corporate law	4.01 (20)	4.98 (10)	+.97**
Medium firm, business law	5.01 (16)	5.80 (3)	+.79**
Small firm, business law	4.86 (17)	5.21 (8)	+.35
Mean for category	4.63	5.33	+.70**
Corporate house counsel	4.26 (19)	4.62 (15)	+.36
Other private firms			
Medium firm, general practice	5.73 (6)	6.40 (1)	+.67**
Small firm, litigation	5.28 (12.5)	5.24 (7)	−.04
Small firm, general practice	6.23 (3)	6.38 (2)	+.15
Mean for category	5.75	6.01	+.26
Self-employed, solo practice	4.64 (18)	3.69 (20)	−.95**

(*continued*)

Table 2.2 *(continued)*

Note: Mean based on ten-point scale; score of ten indicates greatest desirability. N = 103.

[a] The number in parentheses is the rank order for that score in relation to the other mean scores in that column.

* Statistically significant at the .15 level.

** Statistically significant at the .05 level.

Table 2.3 Job Preferences: Changes in High Ratings

	Number at Time 1	Number at Time 2	Absolute Change	Time 2 as Percentage of Time 1
Public interest jobs				
ACLU staff attorney	25	19	−6	76%
Legal aid or services	24	15	−9**	62%
Minority rights organization	21	16	−5	76%
Public defender	25	20	−5	80%
Public interest law center	33	19	−14**	58%
Public interest lobby	38	22	−16**	58%
Small firm—much public interest work	24	21	−3	88%
Total	190	132	−58	69%
Federal social services agency	21	14	−7	67%
Other government jobs				
District attorney	21	21	0	100%
Federal regulatory agency	22	16	−6	73%
State or local agency	16	8	−8	50%
State supreme court clerk	33	27	−6	82%
Total	92	72	−20	78%

(continued)

Table 2.3 (*continued*)

	Number at Time 1	Number at Time 2	Absolute Change	Time 2 as Percentage of Time 1
Business-oriented private firms				
Large firm, corporate law	16	25	+9**	156%
Medium firm, business law	24	38	+14**	158%
Small firm, business law	23	27	+4	117%
Total	63	90	+27	143%
House counsel for corporation	*17*	*21*	*+4*	*124%*
Other private firms				
Medium firm, general practice	23	37	+14**	161%
Small firm, litigation	15	31	+16**	207%
Small firm, general practice	31	39	+8	126%
Total	69	107	+38	155%
Self-employed, solo practice	17	13	−4	76%

Note: Number of respondents rating job eight or higher on ten-point scale. N = 101.

** The difference of proportions for the dichotomized variable (1 through 7 = 0, 8 through 10 = 1) is significant at the .05 level.

interest law center and with a public interest lobbying group. The number of respondents rating each of those jobs eight or higher dropped 42% during the students' stay at the law school; for all seven public interest jobs the decrease was 31%.[8] By contrast, the number of ratings of eight or higher rose 43% for business-oriented law firms and 55% for other private law firms. A strong trend away from a preference for public interest practice and toward conventional practice is clear.[9]

Two previously published panel studies found changes similar to those reported here, suggesting that the data for DU are representative of other law schools. Erlanger and Klegon surveyed students at the

University of Wisconsin at the beginning of their first year (fall, 1973) and at the end of their second year. One set of questions asked the Wisconsin students about the type of job they desired five years after graduation. The proportion whose responses were classified as "social reform" or "social reform, maybe traditional" fell from 38% at the beginning of the first year to 27% at the end of the second year.[10] The students were also asked to rate a list of thirteen work settings on a three-point acceptability scale. The only public interest job on the list, "staff of public defender's office," showed a drop in mean rating of .32, second only to teaching, down .40.[11] Erlanger and Klegon also asked about the students' desire to do *pro bono* work. At the beginning of their law school careers, 26% of the students said that the opportunity to do *pro bono* work would be a very important consideration in their choice of job. By the end of the second year, only 16% gave that response.[12]

Kubly's findings at the University of California, Davis, law school also suggest declining interest in public interest careers.[13] The number of students in the class of 1975 who anticipated jobs as "movement," "poverty," or "public interest" lawyers dropped from 37% at the beginning of the first year to 22% at the beginning of the third year.[14]

Values and Expectations: A First Step in Explaining Change in Job Preferences

As an undergraduate, Allison Smith had majored in social work, answered mail for the American Civil Liberties Union, served as a volunteer probation counselor for juveniles, and canvassed for liberal candidates for political office. In addition, she spent a summer working for an American Indian Center. As a law student, she participated in a Denver Bar Association program providing legal services for the poor.

Allison began law school hoping for a career serving what she described as "human/humane interests." Jobs through which she thought she might accomplish this goal included work as a public defender, American Civil Liberties Union staff attorney, or private attorney with a speciality in American Indian law. The job she considered most preferable from my list of twenty was "attorney for an organization working to protect the rights of racial minority groups, such as the Native American Rights Fund or the NAACP."

Allison's desire to practice law in the public interest hardly wavered during her years in law school. She steadily maintained her desire to work for the disadvantaged and sharpened her initial interest in Indian law. During her final year of law school she used personal contacts and the Martindale-Hubbell directory of lawyers to seek out potential employers of the type she desired. Her persistence paid off with a job clerking for the judge of a tribal court while she studied for the bar exam. After being admitted to the bar, she established a solo practice specializing in Indian law with the tribal judge and the tribe providing her with enough work to stay afloat economically.

A useful way to understand Allison's sustained commitment to public interest law is to focus on the continuity of her values and expectations.[15] By values I mean a person's wants, needs, desires, and drives, and the relative intensity with which they are held. Values shape job preferences in that people are attracted to those jobs most likely to be in accord with their values. For example, a person who greatly values having a high monetary income and cares little about having the opportunity to help the needy will likely have quite different job preferences than a person who values highly the opportunity to help the needy and cares little about having a high income. But differences among various persons' job preferences cannot be accurately predicted simply on the basis of knowledge about their values. One must also have knowledge of their expectations that holding particular jobs will be in accord with, or cut against, those values. For example, two persons might place an equally high value on being challenged intellectually, but they might have different expectations as to which areas of law, or which jobs, provide that challenge.

I measured *values* using a list of twenty-one job attributes (see table 2.4), including such items as "earn a high starting salary," "help persons or groups with whom you identify or sympathize," "challenge your ability," and "control your own work and work schedule." My questionnaire asked respondents to rate each of these job attributes from 1 (less important) to 10 (most important) in terms of its desirability in the person's initial job and, in addition, to rank-order the five most desirable job attributes on the list.

The stability of Allison's values over time is reflected by the fact that the attributes included in her top five did not change between her first quarter in law school and her last. Those five (in rank order from the second questionnaire) were "live in the right geographical locale," "help persons or groups with whom you sympathize," "work for desired social and political goals," "have time to satisfy off-the-job interests," and "earn at least a moderate starting salary."

I measured *expectations* about job characteristics by asking the respondents to indicate on a five-point scale the likelihood that each of the twenty-one job attributes would in fact be found in each of eight specified jobs. Allison's expectations, so measured, were also relatively stable over time, especially with regard to those job attributes

Table 2.4 Values: Attributes Most Desirable in First Law Job

Attributes (grouped by type)	Time 1 Mean Rating	Time 2 Mean Rating[a]	Mean Change in Rating
Salary			
Earn a high starting salary	5.30 (20)[b]	5.28 (21)	−.02
Move to a high future salary	7.25 (16)	7.00 (15)	−.25
Earn at least a moderate starting salary	8.10 (8)	8.26 (7)	+.16
Prestige			
Gain professional and/or community prestige	6.16 (19)	6.23 (18)	+.07
Security			
Have job security	6.36 (18)	6.18 (19)	−.18
Advance with initial employer	5.15 (21)	5.95 (20)	+.80**
Long-term benefits			
Gain valuable experience, knowledge, and contacts	8.50 (3)	8.72 (2)	+.22
Flexibility for future job options	7.59 (11)	7.70 (12)	+.11
Off-the job benefits			
Time to satisfy off-the-job interests	8.45 (4)	8.53 (4)	+.08
Live in the right geographical locale	8.24 (6)	8.45 (6)	+.21
Interpersonal and organizational factors			
Congenial interpersonal atmosphere	8.19 (9)	8.67 (3)	+.48**
Guidance from experienced attorneys	7.50 (14)	8.49 (5)	+.99**
Work directly with clients	7.08 (17)	7.38 (13)	+.30
Control own work and schedule	7.50 (13)	7.96 (10)	+.46**
Craft satisfaction			
Do innovative and creative work	8.23 (7)	7.75 (11)	−.48**

(*continued*)

Table 2.4 (*continued*)

	Time 1 Mean Rating	Time 2 Mean Rating[a]	Mean Change in Rating
Challenge your ability	8.35 (5)	8.24 (8)	−.11
Especially use your legal skills	7.30 (15)	7.22 (14)	−.08
Feel the satisfaction of producing results	8.68 (2)	8.07 (9)	−.61**
Work in interesting areas of law	9.04 (1)	8.78 (1)	−.26
Altruistic goals			
Work for desired social and political goals	7.75 (10)	6.52 (17)	−1.23**
Help persons or groups with whom you sympathize	7.53 (12)	6.70 (16)	−.83**

Note: Mean based on ten-point scale; score of ten indicates greatest importance of that attribute in choice of first job. N = 101.

[a] Time 2 scores were adjusted by adding .21 to adjust for a decrease in mean ratings across all attributes between Time 1 and Time 2.

[b] The number in parentheses after each score is the rank order position (1 = high) of that mean score in relation to the other mean scores for that point in time.

** Statistically significant at the .05 level.

she valued most highly. Given the relative stability of her values and expectations, it is not surprising that her job preference also remained relatively stable over time.

In contrast to Allison, consider the case of Barbara Phillips. Like Allison, Barbara started law school planning to practice public interest law. In answering my first questionnaire, she described her ideal first job out of law school by saying that she "would like to be a partner in a small group of feminist women lawyers, using our skills and resources for the advancement of women." Her preferred job on my list of twenty was "attorney for a 'public interest lobby group' for which you did litigation, lobbying, investigative research, political organizing, and public relations." By her final quarter of law school, Barbara's responses to both my open-ended and closed-ended questions indicated that she wanted to work in the corporate department of a large law firm.

At the beginning of her law school career, Barbara's values were in many respects similar to Allison's. The five job attributes Barbara rated most highly on the first questionnaire were "help persons or groups with whom you identify or sympathize," "have time to satisfy off-the-job interests," "work for desired social and political goals," "live in the right geographical locale," and "work in a congenial interpersonal atmosphere." But Barbara's values changed in an important respect during her years in law school. Three of her top five job attributes remained the same, but "help persons and groups with whom you sympathize" and "work for desired social and political goals" fell from the top five to be replaced by "challenge your ability" and "control your own work and work schedule."

What appears to have happened to Barbara during law school is that she found great satisfaction in conquering the intellectual challenges posed by complex legal problems. Over time, she came to value that intellectual challenge more than the chance to work for social and political goals or to help persons or groups with whom she sympathized. Interestingly, Barbara's political ideology changed hardly at all during law school; her answers to another series of questions indicated that she retained the same strong left-wing views with which she began. Thus, although her views on political issues did not change, her desire to use her position as an attorney to advance her political beliefs changed markedly. By the fall of her second year, this transformation had progressed to the point that Barbara could say, "I don't see being an attorney being an expression of my political beliefs. It's [just] something I'll be good at."

Accompanying this shift in Barbara's values was a shift in her expectations. When she took the basic class in corporate law, she was surprised to find that it was her favorite course. She had imagined that corporate law would be boring but found that, more than any other area of law, it provided her the sort of tough intellectual challenge that she increasingly appreciated. Her expectations concerning the likelihood that employment by a large corporate firm would fulfill some of her most important values shifted accordingly. As Barbara explained,

> I took it [corporations] because it's on the bar [exam], and I found that I really like the area of law. I find it very challenging, very intellectually challenging. I thought for a long time I wanted to do domestic relations, and it's a good area to go into to help people and all that, but it's basically boring. . . . you're basically either doing adoptions or doing divorces. . . . I'm not sure I really want to do that. I really think I'd get a lot of satisfaction out of it but not intellectual satisfaction—not that kind of really brain-teasing challenge. And you find that in corporate commercial practice. That stuff is hard! I mean you're talking about securities work that is really hard to do!

Thus, just as Allison's continuing commitment to public interest practice can be explained by her relatively stable values and expectations, Barbara's shift away from public interest practice can be explained by her changing values and expectations.[16]

In attempting to account for the erosion in desire for public interest practice, many critics of legal education have emphasized the effect of legal education on students' values.[17] The potential impact of changes in expectations has received much less attention. The present study was explicitly designed to assess the effect of both values and expectations as causes of changes in job preferences. The remainder of this chapter identifies the changes in students' values and expectations that are of greatest importance in accounting for the shifts in job preferences illustrated in tables 2.2 and 2.3.

Shifts in Values and Expectations as Reflected in the DU Questionnaire

Values. In the spring of 1977 a sample of then-enrolled DU law students answered a pilot questionnaire asking them to describe the attributes they would most like to find in their first job as an attorney.[18] Their answers were used to construct a list of twenty-one job attributes later used to measure the values of my panel of respondents. As I described earlier, the questionnaires administered at the beginning and at the end of the respondents' law school careers asked each student to rate each attribute on a ten-point scale in terms of its desirability in the first job after graduation.

Table 2.4 shows the adjusted[19] change over time in the mean ratings given each of the twenty-one job attributes and the rank of each attribute based on its mean rating at Time 1 and at Time 2. To further facilitate the analysis of change, the attributes were grouped into eight categories. The items within each category were chosen based on a factor analysis of the individual respondents' changes over time on the attributes.[20]

The two attributes showing the sharpest *decline* in mean rating were those involving altruistic goals. The average respondent's desire to "work for desired social and political goals" in the initial job dropped by 1.23 points between the beginning and end of law school; desire to "help persons or groups with whom you identify or sympathize" dropped by .83 points.[21] Although at the beginning of law school these altruistic goals were rated at about the middle of the list of job attributes (tenth and twelfth, respectively), by the end of law school they were much nearer the bottom (seventeenth and sixteenth).

The attributes showing the third and fourth greatest decline in mean ratings were both among those classified as involving "craft satisfaction." The mean rating for "feel the satisfaction of producing results" fell by .61, dropping it from second to ninth place. "Do innovative and creative work" declined by .48, falling from seventh to eleventh. The mean ratings for the three other job attributes classified as involving craft satisfaction also declined, but the differences were not statistically significant.

Three of the four attributes with statistically significant *increases* in mean rating were those involving interpersonal and organizational factors. While in law school, the students became more concerned with finding a job in which they would "receive guidance from experienced attorneys" (up .99, from fourteenth to fifth position), "work in a congenial interpersonal atmosphere" (up .48, from ninth to third), and "control own work and work schedule" (up .46, from thirteenth to tenth). The fourth attribute with a large increase in mean rating was "advance professionally with initial employer" (up .80, from twenty-first to twentieth). But perhaps just as significant as these relatively large changes is the fact that there were only slight changes over time in the extent to which the students valued attributes involving salary, prestige, long-term benefits, and off-the-job benefits.

In summary, students became somewhat less concerned with finding a job in which they could change the world and help others and a little less enthusiastic about result-oriented, creative work. At the same time, they became somewhat more concerned with securing a "comfortable" job—one in which they could receive needed guidance while avoiding unwanted control, work with friendly and cooperative people, and advance professionally with the initial employer. With only a bit of oversimplification, one might say that during law school DU students decided they were willing to trade some of the excitement and stimulation of helping others or being challenged professionally for increased freedom from certain kinds of on-the-job aggravation, anxiety, and uncertainty. At the same time, the average student apparently did not become more concerned with monetary reward or personal prestige.

Expectations. The students' expectations concerning the twenty-one attributes in table 2.4 were measured for eight of the twenty jobs discussed earlier (see table 2.1). The eight jobs included five public interest jobs and three jobs with conventional law firms. Using a five-point scale, each student rated the likelihood that each of the twenty-one attributes would actually be found in each of the eight jobs—168 such likelihood ratings in all. Respondents indicated whether they would be "much more likely (scored 5)," "somewhat more likely," "about as likely," "somewhat less likely," or "much less likely (scored 1)" to find a particular attribute in the job in question compared to "most other jobs."

Two of the eight jobs for which expectations were measured—small firm with much public interest practice and small general practice law firm—have been eliminated from the present analysis because there were only small changes in the preference for them. The data on expectations for the other six jobs are reported in tables 2.5 and 2.6. Table 2.5 reports the respondents' mean expectation ratings at Time 1 for each of the twenty-one attributes for the six jobs. Table 2.6 reports the mean changes[22] in expectations over time, derived by comparing the Time 1 ratings with those for Time 2.[23]

Not surprisingly, at both the beginning and the end of law school the DU students rated the eight attributes associated with *salary, prestige, security,* and *long-term benefits* as more likely to be found in jobs with both a medium-sized business law firm and a large corporate law firm than in jobs with a public defender, a legal aid office, a minority rights organization, or a public interest law center. However, it is noteworthy that the gap between the four public interest jobs and the two conventional jobs generally widened between Time 1 and Time 2, primarily because of decreases in the scores for the public interest jobs. The mean scores for all eight attributes decreased for both the public defender and legal aid jobs, as did seven of the eight for the minority rights organization and the public interest law center. (Nineteen of these thirty declines in mean expectations score were statistically significant at the .05 level and three more at the .15 level.) For the two conventional jobs, there were some increases and some decreases in the ratings for the eight attributes, but none of the changes were statistically significant at the .05 level, and only four of them were significant at the .15 level.

The story regarding the *altruism* and *craft satisfaction* attributes is different. At the beginning of law school the students expected more opportunities for both altruism and craft satisfaction from the public interest jobs than from the conventional jobs (table 2.5). In fact all four public interest jobs were rated above both the conventional jobs on all seven of the job attributes involving altruism and craft satisfaction. But by the end of law school, important changes had occurred. The public interest jobs still were uniformly rated superior to the conventional jobs on altruism, but the magnitude of the differences had substantially declined, especially with regard to "helping persons or groups with whom you identify or sympathize." The mean scores for the altruistic job attributes declined for all four public interest jobs and increased for the two conventional jobs (table 2.6). Seven of these twelve individual changes were statistically significant at the .05 level, and two more were significant at the .15 level.

The change was also great for expectations of craft satisfaction. The pattern of increasing expectations of craft satisfaction from the conventional jobs was especially clear; eight of the ten individual changes reported in table 2.6 were statistically significant at the .05 level. For three of the four public interest jobs (legal aid, minority rights organization, and public interest law center) there was a clear pattern of change in the opposite direction. For these three jobs, twelve of the fifteen craft satisfaction ratings experienced declines statistically significant at the .05 level, and two more at the .15 level. (For the fourth public interest job—public defender work—the picture was less clear, with only one such decline significant at the .05 level, and one at the .15 level.) As a result of all these changes, by the end of law school neither the public interest jobs nor the conventional jobs were consistently rated higher than the other on craft satisfaction.[24]

The picture is much less clear-cut for attributes related to *off-the-job benefits* and *interpersonal and organizational factors*. At both the beginning and the end of law school, the students expected to find substantially more guidance from experienced attorneys and substantially less direct contact with clients in conventional jobs than in public interest jobs. Beyond that, clear differences between the two types of jobs are not apparent, nor are there clear patterns of change.

The overall picture with regard to aggregate shifts in expectations might be summarized as follows. First, the students' expectations that a job would have attributes they desired generally declined for the public interest jobs and increased for the conventional jobs. The mean ratings dropped on almost all of the attributes for the public interest jobs, while they rose on most of the attributes for more conventional jobs. As a result of these changes, the public interest jobs' initial disadvantage with regard to attributes involving salary, prestige, security, and long-term benefits became even greater over time. The public interest jobs' initial advantage with regard to altruistic goals was reduced but not eliminated, while their initial advantage with regard to craft satisfaction was eliminated but not reversed.

Values, Expectations, and Job Preference: An Analysis of Change at the Individual Level

The changes detailed in the last section—the decrease in commitment to altruistic goals and the decrease in the expectation that public interest jobs would allow the new attorney to achieve altruistic

Table 2.5 Expectations: Mean Time 1 Ratings of Attributes for Six Jobs

Attributes (Grouped by Type)	Legal Aid	Public Defender	Minority Rts. Org.	Pub. Int. Law Center	Med. Firm Bus. Law	Lrg. Firm Corp. Law
Salary						
Earn a high starting salary	1.44 <[a]	1.65 <	1.70 <	2.01 <	3.51 >	4.01 >
Move to a high future salary	1.96 <	2.22 <	2.09 <	2.56	4.19 >	4.52 >
Earn at least moderate starting salary	2.52	3.02	2.50	2.78	3.90 >	4.26 >
Prestige						
Gain professional and/or community prestige	2.50	2.64	3.01	3.32	3.55 >	3.68 >
Security						
Have job security	3.00	3.27	2.75	3.00	3.52 >	3.57 >
Advance with initial employer	2.32 <	2.47 <	2.65	3.06	3.85 >	3.90 >
Long-term benefits						
Gain experience, knowledge, and contacts	2.84	3.16	2.89	3.50	3.47	3.55 >
Flexibility for future job options	3.04	3.22	2.66	3.18	3.47	3.29

Off-the-job benefits						
Time to satisfy off-the-job interests	3.13	2.92	2.89	2.94	3.02	2.94
Live in the right geographical locale	3.31	3.40	2.67	3.19	3.22	2.79
Interpersonal and organizational factors						
Congenial interpersonal atmosphere	3.07	2.69	3.27	3.75	3.01	2.57
Guidance from experienced attorneys	2.77	2.99	2.98	3.28	4.05 >	4.25 >
Work directly with clients	4.65 >	4.56 >	3.75 >	2.87	2.71	2.03 <
Control own work and schedule	2.57	1.94 <	2.99	3.01	2.60	2.19 <
Craft satisfaction						
Do innovative and creative work	3.16	2.85	3.79 >	4.25 >	2.56	2.17 <
Challenge your ability	3.59 >	3.57 >	3.83 >	4.13 >	3.27	3.21
Especially use your legal skills	3.64 >	3.75 >	3.66 >	3.92 >	3.48	3.45
Feel satisfaction of producing results	3.61 >	3.55	3.68 >	3.94 >	2.68	2.25 <
Work in interesting areas of law	3.14	3.06	2.98	3.71 >	2.67	2.32 <
Altruistic goals						
Work for desired social/political goals	3.55 >	3.17	3.97 >	4.30 >	2.07 <	1.85 <
Help people with whom you sympathize	3.60 >	3.34	3.53 >	4.03 >	2.18 <	1.84 <

Note: Mean based on five-point scale; score of five indicates that attribute is "much more likely" to be found in indicated job compared to "most other jobs." N = 103.

[a] Ratings less than 2.50 are highlighted with the symbol <; those greater than 3.50, with the symbol >.

Table 2.6 Expectations: Mean Changes in Ratings for Six Jobs

Attributes (Grouped by Type)	Legal Aid	Public Defender	Minority Rts. Org.	Pub. Int. Law Center	Med. Firm Bus. Law	Lrg. Firm Corp. Law
Salary						
Earn a high starting salary	−.07	−.19**	−.23**	−.22**	+.02	+.20*
Move to a high future salary	−.21**	−.25**	−.28**	−.21**	−.16*	−.08
Earn at least moderate starting salary	−.09	−.21*	−.09	+.01	+.05	+.05
Prestige						
Gain professional and/or community prestige	−.21*	−.15	−.38**	−.29**	+.04	+.18
Security						
Have job security	−.05	−.16*	+.10	−.03	+.04	−.18*
Advance with initial employer	−.09	−.22**	−.10	−.30**	−.13	−.15*
Long-term benefits						
Gain experience, knowledge, and contacts	−.37**	−.55**	−.51**	−.56**	+.01	−.16
Flexibility for future job options	−.29**	−.34**	−.40**	−.37**	−.01	+.16

Off-the-job benefits						
Time to satisfy off-the-job interests	−.13	−.21**	+.09	+.15*	−.14	−.39**
Live in the right geographical locale	−.18	−.26*	−.07	−.32**	+.07	+.22*
Interpersonal and organizational factors						
Congenial interpersonal atmosphere	+.15	+.24*	−.02	−.32**	+.22**	−.08
Guidance from experienced attorneys	−.13*	−.10	−.17*	−.19**	−.19*	−.26**
Work directly with clients	−.10	+.04	−.05	−.02	+.07	−.07
Control own work and schedule	−.06	−.03	−.11	−.24**	+.13	+.07
Craft satisfaction						
Do innovative and creative work	−.20*	−.06	−.32**	−.43**	+.45**	+.58**
Challenge your ability	−.43**	+.06	−.28**	−.45**	+.37**	+.51**
Especially use your legal skills	−.40**	−.14	−.39**	−.51**	+.08	+.07
Feel satisfaction of producing results	+.03	−.34**	−.28**	−.49**	+.24**	+.31**
Work in interesting areas of law	−.24*	−.32*	−.31**	−.51**	+.38**	+.44**
Altruistic goals						
Work for desired social/political goals	−.10	−.15	−.20*	−.33**	+.18*	+.13
Help people with whom you sympathize	−.33**	−.56**	−.36**	−.37**	+.34**	+.32**

Note: Table shows mean change in expectation that attribute will be found in indicated job, based on Time 2 rating (not shown) minus Time 1 rating (shown in table 2.5). N = 103.

* Statistically significant at the .15 level.

** Statistically significant at the .05 level.

goals, perform professionally satisfying work, and develop a productive career—are consistent with the decrease in preference for public interest jobs reported at the outset of this chapter. It remains to be shown, however, that changes in values and expectations about jobs, on the one hand, and changes in job preferences, on the other, are associated on the *individual* level. In other words, are the people who show a decrease in altruistic goals, and/or report changed expectations about the opportunity to realize their values in public interest jobs, the same ones who report reduced preferences for public interest jobs themselves? This section analyzes that issue.

Table 2.7 summarizes the results of a series of exploratory regression analyses, showing the effect of changes in values and expectations on changes in job preferences for the six job settings discussed previously.[25] The left-hand column of the table shows those changes in values and expectations that were used as independent variables in at least one of the six regression equations; the six columns to the right show the results of the regression analyses and the variance explained for each of the six jobs.[26]

For each job, standardized regression coefficients are only shown for attributes that were included as independent variables in the analysis. Attributes were selected by first eliminating those variables for which aggregate change was not significant at the .15 level, and then subjecting the remaining variables to a forward stepwise regression procedure in which only variables with regression coefficients significant at the .15 level were entered in the equation, and only variables with coefficients significant at the .25 level were retained.[27] The results of alternative methods of paring the independent variables to a reasonable number yielded results similar to those reported here.[28]

Five independent variables survive as predictors of change in preference for a job with a legal aid office (table 2.7).[29] The most important *value changes* occur in two areas: the desire to work for social and political goals and the desire to work in a congenial atmosphere. In the aggregate, the importance of working for social and political goals declined markedly, while the importance of working in a congenial atmosphere increased (table 2.4). Since both these variables are positively related to the change in preference for legal aid work (table 2.7), we may infer that these two changes in value orientations worked against each other.

Three *changes in expectations* about what legal aid work would be like are important in predicting change in preference for a legal aid job: (1) the change in the expectation about the opportunity to gain valuable experience, knowledge, and contacts through legal aid work, (2) the change in the expectation that this type of work would challenge the new lawyer's ability, and (3) the change in the expectation that legal aid work would give the respondent the opportunity to help persons or groups with whom he or she sympathized. The expectation that each of these attributes would be present in legal aid work decreased during law school (see table 2.6); the positive coefficients in table 2.7 indicate that these changes are associated with a decrease in preference for legal aid work. Cumulatively, 41% of the variance in the dependent variable—change in preference for legal aid work—is explained by the five independent variables.[30]

Results for the other three public interest jobs are similar. For each, a value change associated with altruism—either the desire to work for preferred social and political goals or to help persons or groups with whom the respondent sympathized[31]—survives as a predictor of the change in preference for public interest work. In addition, for each job, change in the expectation that the job would provide an opportunity to fulfill these altruistic goals—which declined for each of the jobs (table 2.6)[32]—was a predictor of change in job preference, as was change in the expectation that the job would provide opportunities to gain valuable knowledge, experience, and contacts.[33]

Change in preference for a job with a large firm specializing in corporate work poses a sharp contrast to the findings for public interest jobs. The most important *changes in value* are the desire to advance professionally with the initial employer, which is positively associated with change in preference for a job with a large firm, and the desire to work in a congenial interpersonal atmosphere, which is negatively associated. In the aggregate, students came to value both these attributes more highly during law school (table 2.4); the regression analysis suggests that the increased desire for professional advancement made large-firm work more attractive, while increased desire for congeniality made it less attractive.[34]

Three *changes in expectations* predict change in preference for a job with a large firm: (1) that the new lawyer would have a chance to advance professionally with the firm, (2) that there would be opportunities to do innovative and creative work there, and (3) that the results of work at the firm would be satisfying. In the aggregate, expectations about chances for advancement in large firms decreased somewhat during law school, but expectations about the creative opportunities and rewards of the work increased significantly (table 2.6); this suggests that these increases can help to explain the aggregate increase in preference for large-firm practice.

Finally, the results for a medium-sized firm specializing in business

Table 2.7 Changes in Job Preference Explained by Changes in Selected Values and Expectations

	Dependent Variables					
	Change in Preference for Job with:					
Independent Variables	Legal Aid	Public Defender	Minority Rts. Org.	Pub. Int. Law Center	Med. Firm Bus. Law	Lrg. Firm, Corp. Law
Change in desire to:						
Advance with initial employer	[a]					.19
Work in a congenial atmosphere	.16[b]	.14				−.16
Control own work and schedule				−.19		
Work for desired social/political goals	.11	.13				
Help people with whom you sympathize			.19	.15	−.19	
Change in expectation that job listed will facilitate:						
Earning a high future salary		.19				
Gaining professional and/or community prestige			.21			

Advancing with initial employer		.15				.25
Gaining experience, knowledge, and contacts	.31	.27	.29	.47		
Flexibility for future job options		.16				
Opportunity to do creative work						.36
Challenges to your ability	.28				.24	
Satisfaction from production of results						.37
Opportunities to work for desired social and political goals			.23	.31	.23	
Opportunities to help persons or groups with whom you sympathize	.21	.23			.30	
Variance explained by independent variables shown	.41[c]	.47	.33	.38	.45	.47

Note: Based on stepwise regression analysis; standardized regression coefficients are shown. N = 101.

[a] If no coefficient is shown for an attribute, that attribute was not included in the model for this job.

[b] Data on the statistical significance of the coefficents in this table were not accessible.

[c] Squared multiple–partial correlation coefficient for independent variables in the model.

and corporate law indicate that while change in *desire* to help persons or groups with whom the respondent sympathized is negatively correlated with changed preference for this job, the changed *expectation* that the job setting would give opportunities for altruistic work is positively correlated with changes in job preference. This job had the greatest increase in preference rank (from sixteenth to third) in the list of twenty jobs (table 2.2) and the data of tables 2.4, 2.6, and 2.7 suggest that this increase results, in significant part, from a decrease in altruistic sentiments, combined with increasing acceptance of the view that working for a medium-sized business law firm allows one to serve "ordinary people."

Conclusion

In sum, during law school the number of DU students who preferred that their first job be in public interest law declined markedly, and this shift can be explained in terms of changes in the students' values and expectations.

On the aggregate level, the most pronounced change regarding the job attributes *valued* most was a reduction in student desire to work for social and political goals or to help persons or groups with whom they sympathized. A smaller but still clear decline occurred in the importance attached to deriving craft satisfaction from doing innovative and creative work and feeling the satisfaction of producing results. At the same time, the students gained more appreciation for interpersonal and organizational factors such as receiving guidance from experienced attorneys, working in a congenial interpersonal atmosphere, and controlling their own work and work schedule. And in addition, the desire for professional advancement with one's initial employer increased.

In general, the students' *expectations* about their ability to fulfill their values in public interest practice declined, while their corresponding expectations for conventional practice increased. At the beginning of law school, DU students perceived public interest jobs as providing greater opportunity to achieve altruistic goals and craft satisfaction than conventional jobs. But by the end of law school, students had downgraded the opportunities for altruism in public interest law, while upgrading them for business-oriented jobs (in part, perhaps, through a redefinition of worthy beneficiaries), and had come to see the two types of jobs as more similar in their opportunities for craft satisfaction. Moreover, student perceptions of the disadvantages of public interest jobs with regard to salary, prestige, security, and long-term benefits became more pronounced during law school.

These aggregate shifts in values and expectations cannot in and of themselves explain aggregate shifts in job preferences; individual-level relationships must be examined. At the individual level, four types of variables were found to be particularly important in predicting the changes in student job preferences: first, the decline in the value put on professional altruism, demonstrated by the waning desire to work for social and political goals or to help people with whom the respondents sympathized; second, the decline in expectations concerning the extent of experience, knowledge, and contacts available from public interest practice; third, changes in expectations that various jobs would actually allow a lawyer to help persons or groups with whom he or she sympathized or to work for desired social and political change; and finally, changes in expectations concerning the amount of craft satisfaction to be found in certain jobs, especially as manifested in increased expectations that practice with a large corporate law firm would involve innovative and creative work, provide the satisfaction of producing results, and challenge one's ability.

The next two chapters will consider the processes through which these changes in values and expectations occurred.

NOTES

1. The term "job preferences" is used throughout this book in its everyday sense—not in the economist's sense of an underlying utility function that takes into account all job attributes except relative salary level.
2. The less stringent criterion included jobs for government agencies such as the Environmental Protection Agency and the U.S. Department of Health, Education, and Welfare in which an attorney would be required to serve not only underrepresented individuals or interests but competing interests as well. The more stringent coding criteria excluded this type of job.
3. Among those students retaining a preference for public interest law, there was a good deal of shifting in preference from one public interest job to another.
4. Unfortunately, the list of twenty jobs, along with a question asking the respondents to rate their jobs, took up an entire page of the questionnaire, so the question asking the respondents to circle their most preferred job had to be placed at the bottom of the previous page, where it tended to be overlooked. As a result, the nonresponse rate

for this question was 21.4% on the first questionnaire and 19.4% on the second questionnaire. Because of these high nonresponse rates, the comparison made here is not between identical sets of subjects answering the question at Time 1 and Time 2 but between all respondents at Time 1 and all respondents at Time 2.

5. A possible flaw in the research design should be noted. Thirty-three respondents had already accepted jobs at the time they answered the second questionnaire. The psychological theory of cognitive dissonance, developed by Leon Festinger in his work *A Theory of Cognitive Dissonance* (Stanford, Cal.: Stanford University Press, 1957), suggests that part of the change in job preference between Time 1 and Time 2 for those thirty-three respondents may have occurred *after* they accepted their jobs and may reflect nothing more than post-choice dissonance reduction.

   To check this possibility I used responses to a question asking the students to rate each of the twenty jobs in table 2.1 on a ten-point scale in terms of its desirability as an initial full-time job. A third questionnaire on actual job choice, administered in January, 1981, allowed me to identify those respondents (including those who did *not* have jobs at Time 2) whose actual initial jobs corresponded reasonably closely to one of the job descriptions from table 2.1. The jobs of twenty-three of the respondents who had accepted jobs at Time 2, and of twenty-four of those who only later found jobs, matched a job description from the table with a reasonable degree of fit. These two groups were then compared in terms of the change between Time 1 and Time 2 in the ratings they gave for the job from the table which matched their actual initial full-time job. If dissonance reduction were an important influence on the job ratings of those respondents who had already taken jobs at Time 2, then the average change between Time 1 and Time 2 would be noticeably greater for this group of respondents than for the group that did not yet have jobs. The data show that this was not the case. The mean changes in ratings between Time 1 and Time 2 for the two groups were almost identical—an increase of 2.52 for those who had accepted a job at Time 2 and an increase of 2.46 for those who had not. Therefore, post-choice dissonance reduction by those who had already accepted jobs at Time 2 probably does not bias the results of this study.

6. Here and elsewhere, when I evaluated the degree of change over time in the students' responses, I used tests of statistical significance. However, because the students surveyed constitute a population (minus nonrespondents) rather than a random sample, these tests should not receive the same probabilistic interpretation that would apply if they were used for statistical inference. Significance tests are used here simply as rough indicators of differences between Time 1 and Time 2, taking into account the size of the population and the statistical variance in response patterns. Similarly, they are used to

provide a rough evaluation of other statistical measures such as correlation and regression coefficients. For arguments for and against these uses of statistical tests, see Morrison and Henkel, eds., *The Significance Test Controversy* (Hawthorne, N.Y.: Aldine Publishing Co., 1970).

Results significant at the .05 and .15 levels are noted in the tables throughout the book. The .15 level is used in addition to the more traditional .05 level for two related reasons. First, as the only study of job preference to follow a panel of law students for their full three years of law school, this study is clearly exploratory; thus, it would not make sense to restrict the analysis to the .05 level alone when analyzing potentially important changes over time or relationships among variables. Second, the .15 level draws dividing lines that in most cases correspond with my own rough assessments of which changes or relationships are of sufficient magnitude to be substantively (as opposed to statistically) significant. As a general rule, I have used the .15 level in those instances where the analysis requires that I draw an arbitrary line in excluding certain variables from additional analysis. (Editor's note: Measures of statistical significance are based on a difference of means test, but it was not possible to determine whether the tests presumed independent or paired samples. A test for paired samples would be preferred with these data and would yield a larger number of significant differences than one for independent samples.

7. This possibility has been argued by James M. Hedegard, "The Impact of Legal Education: An In-Depth Examination of Career-Relevant Interests, Attitudes, and Personality Traits among First-Year Law Students," *American Bar Foundation Research Journal*, 1979 (1979): 861.
8. The data in tables 2.2 and 2.3 show that the preference ratings for all non-public interest government jobs also dropped substantially.
9. The changes in job preference reported here can be shown to affect economic supply curves for the types of jobs in question. Robert V. Stover, "The Importance of Economic Supply in Determining the Size and Quality of the Public Interest Bar," *Law and Society Review* 16 (1981-82): 455-80.
10. Howard S. Erlanger and Douglas A. Klegon, "Socialization Effects of Professional School: The Law School Experience and Student Orientations to Public Interest Concerns," *Law and Society Review* 13 (1978): 28, 29.
11. Ibid., 30.
12. Ibid., 27.
13. Craig Kubly, "Three Years of Adjustment: Where Your Ideals Go," *Juris Doctor* 6 (Dec., 1976): 34, 36.
14. Corroborative evidence comes from a large-scale cross-sectional study of seven law schools in 1975, in which students were asked to

rate a number of work settings as "desirable," "acceptable," or "not acceptable." The percentages of first- and third-year students scoring some of these settings "desirable" were as follows:

	First-year Students	Third-year Students
Poverty law office	17%	12%
Public interest law office	32%	22%
Public defender's office	18%	13%
Medium firm (10–40 members)	19%	40%
Large firm (over 40 members)	8%	18%

Source: Unpublished data from "Law Student Activity Patterns Project" of the American Bar Foundation, Ronald M. Pipkin, project director.

For cross-sectional data that do not directly tap career preferences but show other important differences between first- and third-year students, see Gregory J. Rathjen, "The Impact of Legal Education on the Beliefs, Attitudes, and Values of Law Students," *Tennessee Law Review* 44 (1976): 95–101.

15. See especially Bernard S. Phillips, "Expected Value Deprivation and Occupational Preference," *Sociometry* 27 (1967): 151–60. Also see, Peter M. Blau et al., "Occupational Choice: A Conceptual Framework," *Industrial and Labor Relations Review* 9 (1956): 531–43; Jullienne Ford and Steven Box, "Sociological Theory and Occupational Choice," *Sociological Review* 15 (1967): 287–99; and Jennifer Haystead, "Social Structure, Awareness Contexts, and Processes of Choice," *Sociological Review* 19 (1971): 79–94.
16. Of course, the brief explanation just provided vastly oversimplifies the stability and change in both Allison's and Barbara's values and expectations. My brief narrative describes only part of the information reflected in their responses to the questionnaires, and at best the questionnaires provide skeletal summaries of complex cognitive and emotional processes. The gaping holes that remain are only partially filled by my interviews and observations. Still, I believe the analysis here provides a useful starting point.
17. See chapter 5. Much previous writing on value change during law school focuses not on the extent to which students value specific job attributes but instead looks at values less proximate to job preference, such as political ideology, sympathy toward business interests, and beliefs concerning the proper professional role of attorneys. But implicit in these arguments is the premise that changes in ideology, group sympathies, or role orientations affect job preferences by affecting the extent to which students value particular job attributes.
18. More precisely, the pilot questionnaire asked respondents to list job attributes that they would like to find and those that they would like to

avoid. However, the negative attributes listed in their answers are easily converted into positive attributes. For example, "I want to avoid a tense interpersonal situation" is the rough equivalent of "I would like to work in a congenial interpersonal atmosphere." The final list of twenty-one attributes is broad enough to include almost all of the responses to the open-ended pilot questionnaire.

19. Between the beginning and the end of law school, the mean rating across all attributes fell by .21. The mean ratings fell for fourteen of the attributes, rose for six, and remained unchanged for one. Six of the downward shifts, but only two of the upward shifts, were statistically significant at the .05 level. If this tendency resulted simply from some overall drop in the students' predisposition to give high ratings—for example, from an increasing "toughness" in evaluating priorities—then it would be appropriate to correct for such a change by adjusting the ratings. In the absence of an alternative explanation for the change, I deemed it prudent to add .21 to each of the Time 2 ratings. The remainder of the analysis in this chapter is based on the adjusted ratings.
20. Factor analysis is a statistical technique used to take a large number of operational indicators (such as my twenty-one job attributes used to measure values) and reduce them to a smaller number of conceptual variables (such as the eight categories in table 2.4). My factor analysis used residualized change scores. In other words, each of the twenty-one job attributes in the analysis was represented by the residuals from the line of regression produced by regressing the Time 2 scores on the Time 1 scores, yielding an indicator of change that holds constant the effects of regression to the mean and other influences of initial position on degree of change. Separate factor analyses of the Time 1 and Time 2 scores yielded results similar to those produced by this method. The varimax method of orthogonal rotation was used in the factor analysis.
21. There was a strong tendency for the students to use the upper half of the ten-point scale in making their ratings—as suggested by the fact that the mean scores for the lowest rated attributes at both Time 1 and Time 2 exceeded 5.00. Thus shifts of .83 and 1.24 points on the ten-point scale suggest a greater degree of value change than might be true if the entire range were used.
22. Most of the changes in expectations were in a negative rather than a positive direction. As with the scores for the values reported in table 2.4, one might suspect that at least part of this shift was the result of an increasing skepticism in evaluating what various jobs have to offer. In the case of the value ratings in table 2.4, I accepted that type of explanation and adjusted the Time 2 scores accordingly, because no plausible alternative presented itself. But in the case of the expectation ratings in table 2.6, there *is* an obvious alternative. Public interest jobs are greatly overrepresented in table 2.6, and it is for those jobs that most of the decreases occur. These decreases are consistent with

the overall decrease in preference for these jobs. While *some* portion of the changes reported in table 2.6 may be the result of an increased general skepticism, it is impossible to estimate reasonably the degree of any such influence. For that reason, the Time 2 ratings for expectations were not adjusted.

23. In tables 2.5 and 2.6, the twenty-one job attributes are grouped according to the same eight categories used in table 2.4. It is important to remember, however, that these categories were derived from a factor analysis of change in values, not expectations. Factor analysis of changes in expectations failed to produce a set of easily interpretable factors.
24. Comparison of each of the two conventional jobs individually with each of the four public interest jobs regarding the five craft-satisfaction attributes yielded twenty cases in which the public interest job was rated higher at Time 2 and twenty cases in which the conventional job was rated higher.
25. Both the independent and dependent variables were the *changes* in the variables indicated.
26. As reported earlier, data were gathered for twenty-one values and for the students' expectations regarding the extent to which each of these values was likely to be realized in each of the six jobs on which the analysis focused. Three decisions affected the way in which these forty-two potential independent variables were used in each of the six analyses.

First, the attribute "work in the areas of law you find interesting" was eliminated from the analysis when preliminary results suggested that many respondents interpreted the phrase as meaning little more than "work in the job that I'd most like to work in." As a result, this variable explained so much of the variance in the dependent variables that it obscured the effects of the other variables.

Second, the number of independent variables was reduced to a manageable number (with regard to each of the six dependent variables) by eliminating those values and expectations for which there was either (1) little or no aggregate change over time or (2) little or no relationship with the dependent variable. The specific criteria used to eliminate these variables were altered in a series of different analyses, and the results were compared. Although the results varied slightly, the central findings were similar in every instance: those changes in values and expectations of greatest overall importance to shifts in preference for the six jobs in question were the change in the extent to which students *valued* opportunities for altruism, and the changes in the extent to which they *expected* the various jobs to provide craft satisfaction, long-term benefits, and the chance to pursue altruistic goals.

Finally, models based on the intuitively appealing notion of multiplying values times expectations (to achieve a measure of expected utility at each point in time) were run but rejected when it was discovered that this method did not increase the proportion of variance explained in job preference, compared to using values and expectations separately in simple additive models.

27. The fact that each variable was represented by both a change score (in order to measure the individual level relationship between change in each independent variable and change in the dependent variable) and by a Time 1 value (in order to control for regression to the mean) complicated the stepwise procedure somewhat. The statistical criteria for entry into or elimination from the regression equation was the level of significance achieved by the regression coefficient for the change score variable. Time 1 variables were added to or deleted from the equation in tandem with the corresponding change score variables.

    Since, as explained above, all twenty-one job attributes were almost certainly positively valued by most respondents, negative relationships between *expectations* and job preference were assumed to be statistical artifacts and not indicative of true underlying relationships. In two of the six analyses, expectation variables thus negatively correlated met the criteria for entry stated in the previous equation but were passed over for the reason just explained. This procedure had little impact on the findings.
28. The alternative methods employed included backwards stepwise procedures and more ad hoc attempts (some theoretically grounded and some purely inductive) to compare various combinations of independent variables. Analyses using residualized change scores to correct for regression to the mean were also conducted and yielded similar results to those which controlled for Time 1 values by including them as separate variables in the analysis. Attempts at data reduction based on factor analysis were rejected, because no clear-cut factor structure emerged with regard to the expectation variables for some jobs.
29. Editor's note: The data necessary to calculate the statistical significance of the coefficients in this table are not accessible.
30. The variance explained is the squared multiple–partial correlation coefficient, which eliminates the effects of regression to the mean by statistically controlling for the effect of the Time 1 scores for values, expectations, and job preference.
31. High intercorrelation between these two values prevented both of them from appearing in any single regression equation. But additional analysis showed that generally one of the two values could be substituted for the other with little effect on the results.
32. A critic could argue that changes in expectations concerning altruistic values have been operationalized so as to include a component of value change. For example, consider the drop in students' expectations that working at the four public interest jobs would allow them to help persons or groups with whom they identified or sympathized.

The intent of the questions used to measure these changes was simply to tap changes in the students' expectations concerning the extent to which particular jobs provide a meaningful *opportunity* to help individuals or groups—for example, a drop in the expectation that legal services or public defender work are effective ways to help the poor. But it is possible that the questions also measured changes in the students' identification with, or sympathy for, particular groups—for example, a drop in sympathy for the poor. In other words, the students' answers possibly reflect not only change in their perceptions of the opportunities to work for particular goals but also changes in the goals themselves.

The possible importance of such value change was explored in an analysis of the relationship between changes in two types of expectations—one regarding relevant group sympathies and political ideology, the other concerning the opportunity to pursue altruistic goals. The analysis showed that changes in group sympathies and political ideology have some effect on changes in expectations of opportunities for altruism with regard to some of the jobs. But in no case are these effects great enough to suggest that changes in expectations of altruism are primarily a product of changes in group sympathies and political ideology.

33. It is important to note that the changes in expectations concerning the extent to which an initial job with a public interest employer would help achieve long-term goals could simply reflect a change in long-term career preferences. As one's long-term career interests shift away from public interest work, the value of experience, knowledge, and contacts provided by an *initial* job in a public interest field would be expected to decline accordingly. Thus this variable may to some extent reflect, rather than account for, changes in job preferences. However, if this were correct, then the expected value of experience, knowledge, and contacts provided by jobs with medium-sized business law firms and large corporate law firms should have risen over time. But the data in table 2.6 show that they did not. Thus the drop in this sort of expectation for public interest work—and the drop in desire for such work—probably at least in part reflects shifting perceptions of the *type* of experience, knowledge, and contacts actually provided by public interest jobs. As the analysis in chapter 4 will more fully detail, law students apparently came to believe during their law school years that the general quality of experience, knowledge, and contacts provided by public interest jobs is inferior to that provided by many other jobs.

34. The data reported in tables 2.5 and 2.6 show that for the six jobs considered, at both Time 1 and Time 2 students gave the lowest rating on congeniality to a job with a large firm.

3 First-Year Crisis, Second-Year Distractions

The Sources of Value Change

Chasing Paper: First-Year Anxiety and the Decline of Professional Altruism

My already messy scrawl degenerated into a nearly indecipherable scribble as I glanced up at the clock. Three minutes more and I could forget everything I ever knew about civil procedure! Outside I could still hear the sounds of Denver's annual St. Patrick's Day Parade, purportedly the second largest in the United States. Earlier in the morning, midway through the exam, the professor had appeared in front of the classroom with two clowns from across the street where the parade was forming, "I just don't want you to feel totally left out," he had joked. At one minute before noon, a secretary from the registrar's office entered the room. As the second hand circled the clock and returned to twelve, she firmly announced, "The examination is over. Stop writing *now*!"

A few minutes later, the conversations among students in the halls had shifted from civil procedure to the coming examinations in torts and contracts, each for eight hours of credit. Some people were talking about the course outlines prepared by study groups in earlier years. A feeling of uneasiness crept over me as I listened. I had only a few days to study for both exams, and my study groups had totally ignored torts to concentrate on contracts. I had been planning to rely on my lecture notes and a commercially available outline for torts, but suddenly they seemed inadequate. I asked Sharon Lollar if she had a torts outline. She said that she had a copy of one that a friend in our class had received from a second-year student who had gotten it a year ago from a student in the study group that had originally prepared it two years ago. It was a copy of a copy of a copy of an original. Reasoning that the course couldn't have changed much in two years, I quickly asked Sharon if I could borrow the outline to add yet another copy to the chain. The outline was at her apartment, about a mile from the law school. She had ridden her bicycle that day so I arranged to meet her at her apartment in fifteen minutes.

As I walked from the law school to the lot where my car was parked, I joined a stream of cowboys, clowns, and brightly uniformed band members from the dispersing parade. Before I had driven a block from my parking lot, I was trapped in a traffic jam of former parade marchers and watchers. As I slowly inched toward Sharon's house my irritation and anxiety increased. I didn't have time to wait! I had to copy that outline and start studying! Seeing a virtually empty street to my left, I turned up it only to find that within a block I was totally obstructed by a barricade of empty horse trailers and pick-up trucks. Sweating and swearing, I made a sharp U-turn and headed back to find another route around the traffic jam. In less than a minute, I encountered a police officer rerouting traffic in a direction directly opposite my destination. Frustrated but undeterred, I tried another route. Within two blocks, I once again ran into a solid wall of horse trailers and pick-up trucks. Resigning myself to the traffic jam, I returned to my original route; an hour after first leaving the law school, I arrived at Sharon's apartment.

The traffic was thinner but still slow as I drove back to the law school to use the copy machines, but my bad luck had only begun. All the copy machines but one were broken, and a line of several students with hundreds of pages to copy stood ahead of me.

Teeth clenched, I raced to the nearest public telephone and checked the yellow pages for copy centers. There was one not far from Sharon's apartment. Outside the law school, I ran through the few remaining parade stragglers to my car. Traffic was back to normal. I sped to the copy center, parked across the street, and bounded toward the door. It was locked! I had forgotten that it was Saturday. My panic dissipated in disappointment, I dejectedly returned to the law school and waited for my turn at the single copy machine. Finally at about 3:30 I returned to Sharon's apartment with her copy.

Back home I sat down with my prize, only to find that it was of little use. I soon realized that trying to digest another student's sense of the material really wasn't very helpful. The explanations weren't nearly as good as those in the commercial outline that I'd been using all year. Within an hour, I abandoned the outline to fix dinner, my first meal since very early that morning. When I started studying again after eating, it was with my lecture notes and the commercial outline. I never returned to the outline that I had spent over three precious hours to obtain.

Such is the mania of a first-year law student during exam week.

During the first year, most students direct their concern and attention almost exclusively to reducing anxiety and coping with the law school program. Their concern with adjusting to the rigors of a strange and demanding environment is so great that they frequently lose sight of more distant objectives. Thus, students whose initial decision to study law was motivated at least in part by the desire to work for political and social change or to help the underprivileged simply quit thinking about these goals as they attempt to meet the daily challenges of the stress-filled first year.[1]

By the beginning of the second year, the anxiety has dissipated for most law students. In the right environment, altruistic goals might return to the forefront of concern for those persons who initially had those commitments. But neither the law school nor the broader legal community provide much support for the norm of professional philanthropy. At the same time, the typical student's perceptual field is filled with messages supporting traditional goals and values. Unless the student finds refuge in a public interest–oriented subculture, any initially strong commitment to altruistic values is not likely to survive the law school years.

This chapter explains value change in terms of students' experiences during their law school careers. In this first part, the focus is on the pressure-packed first year; the second part of the chapter examines the more relaxed second and third years. My argument is that both these periods are central to the process of value change.[2]

Causes and Consequences of First-Year Anxiety. One occasionally hears descriptions of legal education which suggest that the first-year law student's preexisting value structure is systematically dismantled through a brutal hazing process somewhat like military bootcamp. Once students are sufficiently degraded and dehumanized, they become easy marks for those wishing to fill the empty shells with the manipulative, cynical, and avaricious values of the modern lawyer. I found this description of legal education totally inapplicable to the DU experience.

I do not believe that the stress felt by first-year students is the product of an attempt to dehumanize or degrade them, nor do I believe that students are in fact dehumanized or degraded. They frequently are extremely anxious and highly frustrated, but that is a different matter.

Moreover, I do not believe that the anxiety felt by first-year students is necessarily undesirable, or that pedagogically sound practices should necessarily be altered in order to reduce anxiety. A high level of anxiety may or may not be the inevitable result of any rigorous and demanding first-year program. The changes that I will recommend center not on reducing anxiety but on establishing an environment that provides meaningful support and reinforcement for altruistic professional values.

At least five interrelated factors contribute to the high degree of stress felt by most beginning law students. First, the legal neophyte is confronted by the difficult task of mastering a new and confusing body of knowledge. Second, the law school environment provides only minimal feedback regarding success; uncertainty concerning how to study and how much to study remains high for much of the first year. Third, the student is faced by the challenge of the Socratic method of teaching and by the daily possibility of exposure and embarrassment that it presents. Fourth, almost all law students have known academic success throughout their prior careers; yet in law school, half of them must become accustomed to being "below average." This is especially problematic because of the importance of grades to success in the job market. Finally, the first-year students must integrate themselves into a new social environment and may attach added importance to academic performance in an attempt to win the respect of their classmates. All of these factors direct beginning students' attention toward their studies, leaving little psychic energy for long-term concerns.

Like most law schools, DU confronts the typical first-year student with a demanding workload. The first-year curriculum focuses on the reading and analysis of appellate court opinions. The number of pages of assigned reading is not great, but the beginning student finds it extremely difficult. Not only is one confronted with a baffling array of unfamiliar concepts, but he or she must also master new intellectual skills. The student must learn to make sense out of the sometimes incoherent syntax of lawyers and judges, to think with analytical precision, and to distinguish legally relevant passages from the marginally relevant or irrelevant. He or she must acquire a new vocabulary including numerous Latin and French words and phrases, the meaning of which varies according to the context in which they are used.

All of this is made more difficult by the fact that the mastery of each of these skills depends in part upon ability in the others. For example, it is difficult to distinguish the legally relevant from the irrelevant until one understands the simple meaning of the sentences one is reading.

But it is often difficult to pierce the nearly impenetrable veil of judicial syntax without some sense of legally relevant categories and some knowledge of legal vocabulary, neither of which is independently taught but instead is supposed to emerge from the cases. In short, students are asked to read and make sense of appellate court opinions from the first day of class without receiving any previous instruction in the skills needed to complete the task. Thus they feel compelled to read and reread until finally some small glimmer of understanding appears. But this glimmer seems forever accompanied by shadows of doubt and anxiety.

As the weeks pass, first-year students begin to gain control of these skills only to discover that the length of the reading assignments is increasing accordingly. And, as soon as one level of understanding is reached, students learn that there are deeper levels to be pursued. As Sharon Lollar complained,

> I can do a lot of work and still feel like I'm not doing much, whereas in other types of schools I feel like if I work enough I'm going to accomplish something and I'm going to understand it. Here, they give you so much material that you cannot possibly grasp much of it with great depth, and I don't see much point in that.

In the fall of 1977, all first-year, day-division DU students were expected to take courses in contracts, torts, property, decision process, and legal research. Legal research counted for only a single hour of pass-fail credit. Contracts and torts were both two-quarter courses with grades awarded at the end of the second quarter. Thus at the end of the first quarter students received grades only in property and decision process. As a nontraditional course both in content and presentation,[3] decision process was consigned to secondary status in the curriculum by informal student consensus, and midway through the first quarter an unusually large number of students were absent from the course in both mind and body. Thus for the first quarter the only solid feedback was the grade in property and most students felt significant anxiety about their abilities until after the second quarter.

Without feedback, most students remained uncertain as to how to study or how much to study during much of the first year. The most common reaction was to cover as many bases as possible. Most of my classmates supplemented the assigned reading with material from hornbooks—syntheses of the law written by legal scholars—and with various outlines and summaries published especially for law students. In addition, some poured through the American Law Institute's *Restatements* in the areas of contracts, property, and torts, while others studied refresher materials prepared for bar examination candidates. Most joined informal study groups of three to six students, which usually met at weekly intervals to discuss difficult concepts, review earlier material, and prepare outlines for use in studying for examinations.

Objectively, all this probably could be (and often was) accomplished by most students in forty to fifty hours of concerted effort per week, but many still worried that they might not be doing enough. This uncertainty made many students extremely attentive to the behavior of their peers. The process of constantly monitoring the study habits of others, undertaken by each individual student in an effort to reduce anxiety, had exactly the opposite effect for the group as a whole. Ellen Torgeson, for example, complained about the constant barrage of questions from her classmates.

> The people I talk to at school—I sometimes just have to get away from them because they upset me so much. . . . Sometimes I find that they shake me—it's not my confidence; the competition, I guess, will just shake me up. People are asking me, 'What are you going to study? How are you going to study this? How many cases have you read? How far are you on this syllabus?'

Students who felt that they were mastering the material suddenly became anxious upon discovering that they had failed to perform some task deemed important by others. For example, as the second quarter progressed and increasing numbers of study groups produced collective outlines for their contracts and torts courses, a kind of frenzy to produce outlines set in, and more and more groups of students initiated cooperative outlining efforts of their own. Recognizing the possible absurdity of such behavior, some students joked about their own compulsion to monitor and mimic the behavior of others. Nonetheless, many of us had the habit of not leaving the library without first scouring the nooks and corners for secret outliners.

The anxiety of the first year is compounded by the pedagogical method of most law professors. At DU most first-year professors primarily used the traditional Socratic method, in which students are questioned about assigned reading in a dialogue intended to teach the student to analyze cases and "think like a lawyer." Even when employed in its gentlest fashion, the Socratic method produces anxiety. During the fall and winter quarters of the first year, all my professors made a genuine effort to treat students in a compassionate manner. Students who were unprepared were sometimes scolded, but students who were simply confused or flustered were neither reprimanded nor in any other way intentionally humiliated or embarrassed. Nevertheless, most of us were nervous about being called on, anxious to appear intelligent and prepared, and afraid of looking foolish in front of our classmates.[4]

The perceived importance of scholastic performance—and the consequent anxiety concerning failure—undoubtedly was heightened for most students by the desire to impress classmates both in the repartee of Socratic dialogue and on final exams. Many first-year students came to Denver from outside Colorado; most were not married at the beginning of their law school careers and thus could not depend upon spousal support and encouragement.[5] For students cut off from previous sources of primary group support, the desire to succeed in the eyes of their peers probably was increased by a particularly great need to win new friends. Thus the sources of anxiety discussed above almost certainly were compounded for many students by the challenge of integrating themselves into a new social environment.

The typical student reacted to these sources of anxiety by devoting large amounts of time and psychic energy to coping with the daily concerns of law school. In part this effort manifested itself in the sometimes frantic efforts I have described. As might be expected, the perception of many first-year students (including most of those I interviewed) was that they were confronted by an extremely heavy academic workload. Will Goodman grumbled about "working myself half to death." Barbara Phillips complained that the workload diverted her attention from political concerns. And Nelson Fixx observed that "it's certainly more than anybody I've ever met can do."

On the other hand, an apparently smaller group of first-year students felt that the workload was somewhat less than they had anticipated. My own experience was that the regular assignments were short enough to allow ample additional time for supplementary preparation of various types. I did not systematically inquire as to how much time my classmates spent studying, but I would estimate that during the first two quarters of law school, the total time devoted to attending class, reading course-related assignments, and engaging in other activities directly involving the learning of course materials averaged between thirty-five and sixty hours a week for the vast majority of students. A reasonable estimate would place the median at no more than forty-five or fifty hours a week.[6] To at least some extent, the complaints about workload appear to be part of the myth that the incredible difficulty of the first year affirms the professional competence of those who have withstood the "test of fire" and justifies their high monetary compensation.

I do not mean to imply that students intentionally misrepresent the amount of work. For one thing, the frustration and uncertainty of never knowing how much work is enough might lead to a perception of extreme busyness. Even more importantly, the additional efforts to cope with anxiety contribute to the students' feelings of laboring under an intense burden. Even those students who spent fewer than forty-five or fifty hours a week in strict academic pursuits appeared to spend many more hours and large amounts of emotional energy thinking, worrying, and talking about law school. The most tangible evidence of this was in the kind of conversation that predominated at lunch, during study breaks, and in the halls between classes. For the most part, when we were in the law school, we talked about law school. And even outside the law school—at parties or elsewhere—we talked about law school. The topics of such conversation ranged widely; I have already noted the comparison of study habits, progress in courses, and the like. In addition, we frequently discussed the unqualified brilliance or patent stupidity of various faculty members and fellow students, how to respond in class when unprepared, our nervousness about approaching examinations, the impact of law school on our personal lives, and much more. The role of such talk in reducing anxiety appeared to be substantial. My own study group often seemed more like a therapy group; we talked more about law school than we did about law. I particularly looked forward to our meetings because I knew that we would spend the first hour or so joking about the behavior of our professors, our classmates, and ourselves—laughing away some of the preceding week's accumulated tensions.

The bottom line is that first-year students are so consumed with coping with their immediate environment that other matters often recede from the forefront of their concern. This phenomenon—parallel to one observed in a classic study of University of Kansas medical students[7]—undoubtedly affects students' behavior and attitudes in a number of different ways. To cite just one example, some DU students noted with concern that they felt too busy even to walk across the street from the law school to the courthouse to observe real attorneys at work.

The effect most relevant to the present study concerns the value placed by students on using the law to work for social and political change or to help the disadvantaged. During the course of the first quarter, I observed that students simply seemed to stop thinking about these matters as they became increasingly preoccupied with their studies. This change manifested itself both in an eventual absence of "reform-oriented" conversation during my day-to-day contacts with law school acquaintances and in the self-reports of the students I interviewed.

At the beginning of the year, Sharon Lollar had hoped to participate in a Lawyers Guild project in which law students represented needy clients in unemployment compensation hearings, but she abandoned those plans because of "lack of time." When I interviewed her near the end of the first quarter, Sharon observed that her earlier concern with pursuing a career in which she could help others had declined with her immersion in the rigors of law school:

> I'm more confused than before. It's more like I just don't think about it that much. When I first started law school, I had all these ideas about what I wanted to do, and now I just think about coming here and doing the work.

Barbara Phillips felt the same forces at work but attempted to resist them by characterizing them as a tug-of-war between students and faculty:

> I think a lot of people are just saying, 'I want to get through [law school].' And I don't know whether that's just first-year panic or whether being in law school does that to you. . . . I find that I have to do a lot of reading and do a lot of this and a lot of that. I think a lot of it is designed to bog us down. Whether the faculty realizes that or not, I think that's what's going on. I think they're playing games with the workload—trying to make us *think* we're overworked. I think it's a psych game, and I think the faculty is winning.

None of the other students I formally interviewed described this process quite so explicitly as Sharon and Barbara, but some mentioned that law school kept them too busy to get involved in the sorts of political or volunteer activities that they had pursued in previous years. During the second week of classes an organizational meeting of the student chapter of the National Lawyers Guild—the only student group oriented toward all races and sexes that emphasized political and social change—attracted seven persons whom I recognized as first-year students and probably nearly as many others whom I failed to recognize. By the middle of the first quarter I observed no more than one or two first-year students at most Guild meetings. In part this can be attributed to the Guild's alienation of some of its potential constituency with overbearing radical rhetoric, a matter discussed in more detail in chapter 6. But part of the decline in attendance almost certainly resulted from the reduced importance of political and social concerns for students who were overwhelmed by the intensity of the first year of law school.

Other Factors Affecting the First Year. Other factors in the law school environment also contributed to the decline in salience of altruistic values during the first year. As I noted in chapter 1, most DU law professors did not mention the professional obligation to serve the needy. In only one of my first-year classes did the professor clearly attempt to impress upon us the importance of professional legal service in the public interest, and the total time devoted to such efforts in that two-quarter class cannot have exceeded ten or fifteen minutes. In what may have been an attempt to serve as a role model, the professor in my second quarter of property law described his own activity some years earlier on behalf of needy tenants but gave no indication that his *pro bono* efforts had continued beyond that point. On the other hand, only one of my first-year professors actively discouraged *pro bono* practice, once or twice briefly disparaging "cause-oriented litigation."

Perhaps more important, a number of alternative—although not necessarily competing—values *were* stressed. At the most obvious level, the academic and professional importance of systematic, analytical thought was emphasized. At a more subtle level, most professors placed a repeated, if unintentional, emphasis on the pecuniary aspect of legal practice. Perhaps the most telling manifestation of this tendency was in the use of classroom humor. In at least four of my first-quarter courses—contracts, torts, property, and legal research—the professors joked about the relationship between legal skills and economic success. For example, in my legal research class, the professor frequently closed his discussion of the reasons for a particular research technique by saying something like, "And besides, you'll make a lot more money if you do it that way." Invariably we all laughed. The pervasiveness of this humor is confirmed by the fact that it was frequently mentioned by the students I interviewed. Commenting on her first-quarter classes, Ellen Torgeson, for example, remarked:

> Think about the jokes. Some of the jokes have been money-oriented, and everybody just laughs. I laugh, too. It's not like I think that's disgusting or anything. But it's true. It's just an attribute that everybody assumes.

Perhaps surprisingly, this "green humor" was quite common among those professors who appeared to be the most politically liberal. One explanation for this might be that these professors were consciously or subconsciously trying to build rapport with less liberal students by emphasizing that "liberals are human, too." Another possible explanation is that they were in fact attempting to poke fun at the legal profession's excessive concern with money. But if they were, the students I interviewed did not interpret it in that way. The students believed that they were being told that money is *and should be* important to lawyers. Perhaps the humor cut in several different directions and we laughed so hard at these jokes because they provided us with so many different targets for laughter—"money-grubbing" lawyers; ourselves as somewhat embarrassed future "money-grubbing" lawyers; our future clients as unwitting victims.

My point is not that most DU students necessarily adopted this concern with money. The quantitative data reported in chapter 2 indicate that, on the whole, the level of concern with money remained essentially unchanged during law school. Instead, my point is that the lack of emphasis on altruistic values was accompanied by an undercurrent of support for alternative values that may have helped divert attention away from altruistic concerns. The emphasis on attractive alternatives presented by the students' environment grew even greater during the second and third years of law school.

Law Student, Law Clerk: Professional Culture and the Decline in Professional Altruism

I buttoned my jacket and pushed my chilled hands into my pockets as I walked through downtown Denver from the bus stop toward the law school. The sky was grey and a light mist hung in the air—unusual weather for October. As I walked, a feeling of envy crept over me. My classmates from the year before were in their second year of law school,[8] and I was falling behind, teaching full-time in Boulder, unable to resume my legal studies until January.

Half a block from the law school, I met a friend from my first-year class. She was on her way to a downtown law firm where she worked as a clerk. As we talked, she described the joys of being a second-year student: the feeling of being in control, less need to prepare for class, the time (and skill) to earn money and learn about the actual practice of law through outside employment.

The difference between the first and second years has been noted by previous observers,[9] but I did not truly appreciate the starkness of the change nor its full impact on the attitudes and behavior of law students until that day in October, 1978, when I made my first visit to DU since the preceding June. The contrast struck me almost immediately upon entering the law school. As I greeted old friends, I noted that some of the men wore coats and ties, and more of the women than before wore skirts and blouses, appropriate attire at the law firms where they clerked. In the library I saw a few familiar faces, but whereas the year before the members of my class had dominated the study tables, now the room was full of unfamiliar faces, undoubtedly those of the current first-year students.

As the day progressed, I noticed a marked change from the previous year in the topics of conversation. The constant preoccupation with course work—with workload, with understanding the material, with professors and classmates—was gone. People talked about their jobs with law firms, their work on one of the student-edited legal journals, or even their personal lives. Classes were mentioned frequently, too, but usually to note flippantly that the speaker hadn't started the reading yet or to complain about a professor.

Formal interviews, additional visits to the law school that quarter, and my observation and experience as a second-year student during the winter and spring quarters of the second year confirmed my primary observations of that October day: the stress and anxiety of the first year had been replaced by self-assured confidence; the almost obsessive concern with courses, professors, grades, and fellow students had been replaced by an outward-looking desire for practical experience clerking for law firms, working in the law school's clinical program, or laboring for the *Denver Law Journal*, the *Denver Journal of International Law and Policy*, the *Transportation Law Journal*, or the *Administrative Law Review*.

One key to these changes is that the academic workload drops drastically for most students after the first year. If the informal and formal reports of numerous classmates are even moderately accurate, many, but not all, second- and third-year students substantially reduce the time they spend in academic pursuits. For example, in the fall of her second year Betsie Pierce told me,

> I don't think there's nearly as many people that are putting time into sitting in the library . . . and typing out these outlines and the whole bit. I mean I really think that fades out. . . . I know personally the amount I put into law school is maybe a third of what it was last year because I work . . . twenty-five hours a week almost. And you know, I might have missed some cases—I missed some cases and maybe some relevant information—but I know I'll get through.

By the second year of law school, most students have mastered case analysis. Many have concluded that reading cases is at best boring or at worst a waste of time. Will Goodman told me that he only did the reading in the classes where he thought he might be called on. Nelson Fixx reported that he was doing the reading in only two of his five fall-quarter courses. Jenny Landis explained that

> I take it a lot more casual than I used to. I don't know if the courses are really easy or if it's just as much my attitude as it is that. . . . I talk to people who . . . try to read the textbook. I don't understand how they do it. . . . I just use a hornbook.

Some DU students, content to rely on legal outlines, summaries, or hornbooks, didn't even bother to purchase the assigned casebooks for some courses. Other students pursued the strategy of doing the assigned reading (or reading outlines) but cutting most of their classes, especially if the professor was viewed as a particularly bad teacher. Barbara Phillips described to me the shock exhibited by one part-time professor who appeared at his final exam to discover that not twenty but sixty students were still enrolled in his course. Some of my classmates said that they spent no more than twenty hours a week attending and preparing for their courses. On the other hand, other students maintained a strong commitment to course preparation, continuing to devote forty hours a week or more to course-related work.

Equally noteworthy was the almost total elimination of anxiety about academic performance. For example, in the fall of his second year, Will Goodman was taking seventeen hours of course work and devoting large amounts of time to working for the *Transportation Law Journal*. But in contrast to the previous year, he no longer felt burdened by the workload:

> I don't feel that I'm pressed. I don't know why—maybe a different attitude, maybe I'm better organized, which I doubt, or maybe I'm just doing something I like better.

All of the students I interviewed noted the decline in the pressure. Some had a more clearly developed theory than Will as to what accounted for the change. Ellen Torgeson, who said that she was spending about forty hours a week on course work in the fall of the second year, emphasized that she had developed study techniques that she could count on to yield satisfactory results.

> I have these little methods now, outlining the course. I didn't do that at first. It may take a lot of time, but that's just something that works for me, just different study methods.

The students' security in knowing that their individual methods and routines for studying produced satisfactory grades was probably the most important factor behind the reduced anxiety of the second and third years. Complementing this security born of success was the fact that some students lowered their definition of success to correspond roughly to their first-year performance. In a fairly typical illustration of this phenomenon, one student explained his lack of class attendance this way:

> When I came here from———College, I had visions of being at the top of our class. Well, I know now that's not in the cards, but I'm happy with my 82 average, and I'd rather concentrate on my clerking job than bust my butt worrying about grades.

In addition, the threat of the Socratic dialogue largely disappeared in the second year. Recognizing that the pedagogical utility of that method is greatly reduced for students who have learned to "think like a lawyer," many of my professors abandoned or curtailed its use in second- and third-year courses, content to punctuate their lectures with occasional questions for the students. Professors who employ the Socratic method in second- and third-year courses must face the fact that many second- and third-year students have overcome their embarrassment in stating that they are not prepared or have improved their ability to provide marginally acceptable answers after quickly scanning a case during class. A few students have learned the Socratic method so well that they can defend against it by turning many questions back on the professor with a query of their own so penetrating that it begs for a professorial response.[10] Finally, anxiety was reduced by the fact that most students had now found a group of friends to provide the primary group support that they may have lacked earlier in their law school career.

Thus, in contrast to first-year students, second- and third-year students are not consumed by the demands of law school. As a result, many of the student concerns which had receded during the hectic first year reappeared in the more relaxed atmosphere of the second year. To take just one example, some students reported that their romantic involvements increased. In addition, many second- and third-year students recaptured an earlier desire to observe, understand, and participate in the day-to-day activities of practicing lawyers. This thirst for practical knowledge was quenched not only through part-time legal jobs and the law school's clinical program but also through observation of lawyers at work in the trial courts across the street from the law school and in the state appellate courts only a short distance away. Closely related to this, most second- and third-year students regained their previous concern with career alternatives, using their clerking jobs, clinical experience, and observation of lawyers at work to evaluate future job options.

But despite the reactivation of numerous pre–law school interests and concerns, many of the students who had begun their law school careers with a commitment to altruistic professional values, and had seen that commitment fade during the first year, did not regain it in the second year. A large part of the explanation for this permanent lessening of interest lies, I believe, in the milieu of the law school and the legal community. While the law school and the broader legal community provide support for traditional values, neither provides much support for altruistic values. In the absence of a supportive environment, altruistic values simply are not rekindled in many students but instead are replaced by other concerns. The remainder of this chapter elaborates this explanation.

Professors and Students. The way in which the law school's failure to support altruistic values affects students' choice of jobs is illustrated by Sharon Lollar's drift away from public interest practice. Conscientious and compassionate, Sharon had worked as a caseworker for a state welfare agency and had begun graduate study in social work before switching to law. In answering my first questionnaire, she had said she hoped to "become involved with the ACLU" in her first job as an attorney. When I interviewed her near the end of her first quarter of law school, she said, "I know much more what I don't want to do than what I want to do. I don't want to work for a large corporation or in business-type law, but I think I'd like to do something that's more client-oriented. I've been thinking about legal aid–type work."

By October of her second year, Sharon's job preferences were shifting toward practice with a private law firm. In describing the job she would most like upon graduation, she said,

> It's changing for me because . . . . I'm thinking more on the lines of a small firm doing . . . I don't know . . . not necessarily any sort of specialty. But I'm getting more interested in property law—stuff like that. . . . I've pretty much changed my mind from doing a poverty law–type of thing to doing whatever comes in the door.

By the end of her third year, Sharon was still hoping to find a job with a small law firm with a general civil practice.[11]

Sharon clearly recognized the change she was undergoing and spent a good deal of time contemplating and accounting for that change. She appeared to be unusually able to analyze objectively her own shifting motivations, and her analysis sensitized me to many of the issues I develop in this chapter.

One point that Sharon emphasized was the sharp contrast between the support for altruistic values in law school and in the graduate social work program:

> When I was in social work school, . . . it was client-centered, and you really thought about the issues that affected *people*, and law school just isn't oriented in those terms. And so I think you can't help realigning your thinking.

With a small number of notable exceptions, primarily in classes with an obvious public interest emphasis (such as poverty law), the norm of professional altruism was ignored in second- and third-year courses, just as it had been during the first year. Most surprisingly, my course on the legal profession devoted a full quarter to the study of the Code of Professional Responsibility without once directly confronting the Code's statement that "every lawyer, regardless of professional prominence or professional workload, should find time to participate in serving the disadvantaged."[12] The matter of service in the public interest arose only indirectly, as when the point was made that legal aid attorneys may publicize their availability to clients with minimal risk of breaching the rules prohibiting the solicitation of clients.[13]

In my legal profession class, to the extent my professor revealed his opinions on questions of professional and public concern, they seemed to be "liberal" or "progressive." Had a student asked him to express his views on the importance of professional service on behalf of the underrepresented, he very likely would have strongly endorsed the norm of professional altruism. If this is true, then why did he and many others like him fail to express their beliefs on this matter in the classroom?

I can only speculate, but I think at least part of the explanation lies in the deeply rooted norms of traditional legal pedagogy. Christopher Columbus Langdell, the father of the case method of legal study, assumed the deanship of the Harvard Law School in 1870. By the turn of the century, the Harvard technique of legal instruction, with its pretensions about the scientific character of case method, was ascendant in American legal education.[14] Although not immune to challenge and change, Langdell's prescription for proper legal pedagogy maintains a surprisingly strong hold on the collective consciousness of the legal professoriate. Today most law professors probably do not believe that law is quite the science that Langdell believed it to be, but hardheaded, deductive reasoning is still prized, and fuzzy-minded, muddled thinking is still abhorred. Students must be taught to "think like lawyers," and for at least some law professors this means teaching them to "overcome the blinders" of ideology and sentiment—teaching them to leave their normative concerns at the classroom door just as they must later leave them at the courtroom door.

My impression was that many of my professors probably did not see a clear-cut incompatibility between normative concerns and hard-headed analytical thinking. At the same time, however, they might have felt constrained by what they *perceived* as the accepted proprieties of classroom behavior. In all probability their own professors had not stressed normative concerns, and, to the best of their knowledge, their colleagues at DU probably did not stress it either. As a result, even those professors with a strong commitment to professional altruism may have felt that the overt expression of opinion on the issue would not be in keeping with professorial norms.

Furthermore, most professors probably were aware that any attempt to lecture second-and third-year students on the importance of *pro bono* service almost certainly would have met resistance. While first-year students may listen intently to a professor's occasional lapse into moral, philosophical, or policy-related issues, the second- or third-year students typically react to such a breach of conventional behavior by putting down their pens—and perhaps also by rolling their eyes in disgust, whispering to a neighbor, or staring into the distance. By the second year, most students have learned that in law school *legal* analysis, narrowly defined, is what matters. Everything else is peripheral. Ethical and normative concerns have been clearly labeled as unimportant by the words and actions of their first-year professors. Not only are such matters largely ignored in the classroom; they are totally ignored on final examinations and almost totally ignored on the bar examination. On several occasions I heard angry complaints about professors who briefly deviated from their normal routine to consider normative issues. For example, in a class populated primarily with first-year students, a third-year student disgustedly reacted to the professor's attempt to discuss the social importance of exclusionary zoning by muttering, "We're not paying for this stuff. I've got to take the bar exam, and he's wasting our time on policy."[15]

This student's attitude is but an extreme version of the majority student sentiment at DU. Even in the fall of the first year, about half of the altruistically oriented students I interviewed expressed the feeling that they were in a tiny minority, and by the second or third year there was universal agreement that students with a public interest orientation were vastly outnumbered by persons with more materialistic concerns. At the beginning of her second year, Sharon Lollar commented on the effect that had on her, reporting that she did not feel comfortable discussing her preference for public interest work in front of other students. She saw a marked contrast to the environment of the graduate social work program in this regard. My own observations confirmed the fact that even those students oriented to public interest concerns did not generally express their views to other students. The professional obligation to serve the disadvantaged for the most part simply did not enter the universe of student discourse at the law school.

The only clearly noticeable exceptions to this pattern occurred within two small overlapping law school subcultures—the student chapter of the National Lawyers Guild and the Student Law Office, where law students represented indigent criminal defendants in misdemeanor-type cases as part of the law school's clinical education curriculum. The role these subcultures played in insulating altruistically oriented students from the effects of the dominant student culture is discussed in chapter 6. For present purposes the main point is that even the students most heavily immersed in these subcultures communicated support for professional altruism almost exclusively to each other. Some of these students appeared to remove themselves from the broader student community during their second and third years, for example by spending long hours at the Student Law Office, eating lunch away from the law school, and skipping large numbers of classes. But others did not—choosing instead to mix and converse with a broad spectrum of students in class, in the library, in the halls, and in the law school snack bar. In such settings, however, these students were not likely to communicate support for public interest values. One reason for this was that attempts to voice support for professional altruism outside the friendly confines of a sympathetic subculture often met with silence or other forms of subtle disapproval, perhaps because they were interpreted as displays of moral superiority. Rather than risk such disapproval from potentially unsympathetic listeners, it often was easier to remain quiet. Louie Littell's description of this phenomenon was perhaps somewhat exaggerated, but it illustrates the point.

> The enemies I've made in law school probably have been the most vehement that I've ever run across in my life. I stand on the premise it's not me, it's them, and so now I have a dual existence. . . . I realized in coming through law school that you've got to watch your politics and watch what you say in front of certain people. . . . I think . . . that has affected the way I deal with things here. I look at school life on one hand and my outside life on the other now. And that's tricky, but it's the healthiest way I can play it.

The result of Louie's withdrawal from discourse on "sensitive" topics was that sympathetic as well as unsympathetic classmates were shielded from his opinions. Writ large across the law school, the net effect of such behavior by people like Louie was that students not in contact with a public interest subculture received little peer support for the norm of professional altruism.

The Impact of Part-Time Legal Work. The absence of support for professional altruism in the law school environment apparently was duplicated in the work environments of most second- and third-year students. Ninety-six of the 103 students who responded to my questionnaires held at least one law-related job outside the law school at some point in their law school careers. The students' responses to the second questionnaire included descriptions of 194 such jobs.[16] Fifty-eight percent of these jobs were with private law firms or solo practitioners, and 75% of the respondents listed at least one job with a private firm or solo practitioner. Only 21 of the 194 jobs listed were with private or governmental organizations specifically devoted to the practice of public interest law—for example public defender and legal services offices, the Mountain States Legal Foundation, and the Native American Center. These 21 jobs were held by 19 students, or less than 20% of the class.[17]

The best available evidence suggests that most practicing attorneys demonstrate little support for professional altruism, in either their attitudes[18] or in their behavior.[19] There is no reason to suppose that Denver area attorneys are atypical in this regard. Moreover, these attorneys may have communicated to their student employees the relatively low esteem in which public interest practice is generally held by members of the bar. According to Laumann and Heinz's study of Chicago lawyers, even with other factors held constant, "the higher a (legal) specialty stands in its reputation for being motivated by altruistic (as opposed to profitable) considerations, the lower it is likely to be in the prestige order."[20]

The substance of the work that student employees are sometimes required to do may also contribute to the decline in altruistic values. Most student law clerks are not in a position to choose their cases. Thus students committed to serving the economically disadvantaged, consumers, or environmental interests sometimes found themselves working "on the other side."[21] In the fall of their second year, Sharon Lollar, Barbara Phillips, and Nelson Fixx all expressed certain reservations about the type of work they were required to do. Barbara was affected to the point that she was concerned that her initial commitment to public interest goals could be in jeopardy.

> There are days when I think I'm wavering. I have a lot of doubts about my clerkship job, which is with a small firm that does primarily corporate practice. And I have a lot of objections about working for corporate clients. Some of the things that we do—none of them are illegal—it's things that I politically object to. . . . I would like to think I could stand firm on my principles, but I'm feeling I could rationalize in a way how my little part in this case couldn't hurt.

In a sense, Barbara may have already been rationalizing, as she went on to emphasize that her top-rate on-the-job training would ultimately serve interests more compatible with her political beliefs. Similarly, Nelson Fixx may have been rationalizing when he implied that after graduation he would be able to choose his own cases.

> I think that right now, not being licensed to practice law and not having enough personal or financial power to pick who I work for makes more difference. . . . When one thinks of only representing the good or only taking cases that one really believes in, you have to assume power to be in a position to make a choice, and the law clerk in Denver in 1978 doesn't have that. He or she is at the bottom of the pile. . . . You don't have any options, or not many. You have [only] an original option in deciding who you're going to work for.

But this dilemma is not unique to the student law clerk; it also exists for the young attorney seeking employment. My point is not that the choice to bend to the pressures of the situation represents a "cop-out." Rather I wish to stress that in order to understand the process of value change, one must be attentive to the likely attitudinal consequences of choosing to work "temporarily" for interests incompatible with one's public interest values.

For example, the theory of cognitive dissonance[22] suggests that student law clerks who make such a choice might eventually alleviate post-choice regret by reducing or qualifying their support for public interest values and by increasing their support for alternative values. Perhaps at first they can reduce psychological dissonance by selectively perceiving or misperceiving reality—by telling themselves that they are merely training for later service in the public interest or that they will be free to choose their own cases as an attorney. But as time goes on, and the number of decisions to work for interests incompatible with their original values accumulate, they may find that they can achieve psychological consonance only by deemphasizing the importance of using the law to work for social change or to help persons or groups with whom they sympathize. By the end of their third year, Nelson, Barbara, and Sharon had abandoned their earlier plans for public interest practice. The psychological need to cope with the discomfort occasioned by the requirements of their jobs as law clerks may have played some part in the change.

Support for Alternative Values. The absence of an environment supporting altruistic values during the second and third years of law school was accompanied by continued support for a number of alternative values. For example, in varying ways and to varying degrees the students were encouraged to maintain or increase the importance attached to analytical thinking, monetary rewards, professional prestige, and career advancement. As before, my point is not that the students' support increased for all or even most of these alternative values. It is simply that reinforcement for these values, combined with lack of reinforcement for altruistic values, may have helped to reduce the chances that altruistic values would return to the forefront of concern for those students who previously had been motivated toward public interest practice.

Classroom emphasis on systematic, analytical thinking continued from the first year into the second and third years with one significant change. Whereas during the first year the professors had sometimes been very explicit about the importance of analytical precision, by the second year it was simply taken for granted. The impact of this continuing emphasis on intellectual rigor appeared substantial. Both my formal interviews and my informal conversations and observations suggested that a number of DU students developed a deep appreciation for the satisfaction to be derived from applying their analytical skills to intellectually challenging legal problems. Furthermore, in some cases this shift seems to have had a fairly direct impact on job preferences. For example, Sharon Lollar helped explain her shift away from public interest practice as follows:

> I think that my original choice of jobs was based on sort of a 'helping the other people' attitude, and that was like the prime thing. And now it's more—I think I'm more interested in getting something that's intellectually stimulating for myself.

An even more marked shift in that direction occurred in Barbara Phillips, as described in chapter 2. According to Barbara, only a major corporate practice could provide the intellectual challenge she desired. Many students such as Barbara began law school with strong analytical aptitudes, honed their skills to meet the specific requirements of legal reasoning, and reaped the rewards that law school offers the intellectually gifted—the praise and respect of professors and peers, an invitation to work on the law review, and broadened career opportunities.

At the same time, students who began law school with scant background in systematic, analytical thinking and little confidence in their analytical abilities also learned the rewards of solving legal puzzles. Ellen Torgeson, for example, began law school with a sense of unease about legal reasoning, in spite of her prior work as a legal secretary for Legal Services. After the first quarter of law school she told me,

> Law school stresses a certain kind of analytical mind that they are trying to form—they are trying to mold you into. And I don't have a very analytical mind at all. I felt like that's something that makes me uncomfortable. . . . I've never done anything like law school. I was an art and music student, and so I wasn't even in philosophy or English. I just have a different style of thinking, and I thought they're trying to teach me this one style, and it seems like it's a narrow thing they try to push me into, but I have to do it to get through school. And I feel very rebellious about that.

By the end of her third year, Ellen's evaluation of her analytical abilities and of the value of analytical thinking had been transformed. She praised her courses on corporate law and the Uniform Commercial Code because they facilitated systematic thought. As she said with only slight caricature when describing the Uniform Commercial Code,

> I love all the little sections, how they fit together, working with them and knowing, OK, it's this, so we look under here—[Section] 7-11—and there's the remedy!

The subtle but pervasive emphasis on the importance of monetary reward that the DU students commented on during their first year also continued into the second and third years. My overall impression was that although the classroom humor about the subject of money abated somewhat, more explicit professorial references to the importance of money, professional prestige, and career enhancement and advancement slightly increased during the second and third years. For example, the adjunct professor who taught my course on negotiable instruments occasionally reacted to questions or comments concerning legal problems likely to be encountered by the common man, and for which high fees would not be appropriate, by disparagingly referring to "that kind of practice." The same professor reinforced the point—and emphasized his own monetary success as an attorney—by mentioning that he sometimes referred such cases to former classmates with "less successful" practices.

On the whole, however, the importance of money and prestige and the career advantages attached to working for the very wealthy were more frequently conveyed more subtly. For example, illustrations drawn from professors' own law practices more often than not involved rich or powerful clients or substantial awards of monetary damages. Similarly, many of the hypothetical examples used in class implied an extremely affluent clientele. In my basic taxation class, the numbers on the chalkboard invariably were far greater than the dollar amounts likely to be encountered by the general practitioner attending to the tax needs of typical middle-class or even upper-middle-class clients. Other professors based some hypotheticals on the problems likely to be encountered by average citizens, intermittently lamenting that the rewards accruing to the client probably would not justify the hiring of an attorney in the first place. No one suggested a personal or collective professional obligation for members of the legal profession to endure some financial sacrifice in attempting to help solve the problem.

The importance and prestige of working for a large law firm in the service of the wealthy was also communicated to the students by their peers. Some students appeared to value the prestige of such work far more than they cared to admit. For example, some would only sheepishly admit to having had job interviews with one of Denver's top corporate law firms and then only with a disclaimer such as, "I'm only going through the interview for the experience," or "If I get an offer I probably won't take it, but if I do, it will only be for a couple of years." But the tone of their voices revealed the pride they felt in having earned an interview with such a firm.

During the three years of law school, a sometimes indistinct, but nevertheless important, academic pecking order developed. Students at the top of the class or those who held an editorial position on the *Denver Law Journal* were generally respected for their success, and a few of these students clearly considered themselves part of an emerging elite. Among the law reviewers and others at the top of the class, the pull of professional prestige was especially great. A job with a large, powerful law firm was one of the acknowledged rewards of academic success. As Barbara Phillips put it, "It's very prestigious, it really is—especially when you beat out people from Harvard." For those with a real chance at such a job it was extremely difficult not to be caught up in the competition. One such student, seemingly firmly committed to a career serving the interests of ordinary people, surrendered to the allure of the large law firm only after failing to get an offer from his first few interviews. My impression was that had he received an offer earlier, he might have felt secure enough in his place at the top to turn it down and pursue his original interests. However, having been rejected as not good enough, he felt compelled to find a job comparable to those taken by his friends on the law review.

The importance of money, prestige, and career advancement were also conveyed to the students by the private attorneys for whom they clerked. According to Allison Smith,

> The first comment made to me, after I came back from being gone this summer, by the youngest attorney [in the law firm] was . . . 'We really made a lot of money.' The one man in this office that makes $130,000 just off his practice—plus investments, plus he is independently wealthy—loves to tell me each week how much money he makes, and this oil well is coming through well, and this client paid us this much, and that sort of thing.

It is not unreasonable to speculate that for some students, the influence of attorney-employers exceeded that of professors and peers.[23]

Thus the absence of support for altruistic values in the students' law school and law clerking environments was complemented by the presence of support for a number of different values. While these were not always antithetical to a desire to work for political and social change or to help the underrepresented, the emphasis they received may have so occupied the perceptual field of some students that it reduced the chances that the altruistic concerns with which they started law school would return.

Conclusion

The need to cope with the daily pressures of the demanding first-year curriculum left students with little time or psychic energy for other concerns, including working for social and political change or providing legal assistance to members of underrepresented groups. But most of the effects of the beginning students' coping strategies were only temporary, and by the second year, most DU students were at ease with their environment and eager for challenges extending beyond the academic study of law. One might expect that at this point, altruistic goals would return to the forefront of concern for most of those students who began law school committed to working for reform and helping others. But neither the law school nor the broader legal community provided much support for the norm of professional altruism. Instead, students were exposed to an environment that supported a broad range of different goals and values which came to occupy the forefront of their concern, and for many altruistically oriented students, the return to public interest values never occurred.

NOTES

1. Recent studies of anxiety in law students include G. Andrew H. Benjamin, et al., "The Role of Legal Education in Producing Psychological Distress Among Law Students and Lawyers," *American Bar Foundation Research Journal* 1986 (1986): 225–52, and Stephen B. Shanfield and G. Andrew H. Benjamin, "Psychiatric Distress in Law Students," *Journal of Legal Education* 35 (1985): 65–75.
2. This is not the only possible approach to explaining value change. One alternative I considered was an analysis of the effect of changes in political ideology, group sympathies, and professional role orientations on changes in altruistic values. That approach did bear some fruit (see chapter 5), but I have emphasized student experiences because cause and effect is easier to establish than when one uses some value changes to explain others, and because the educational experience is a causal factor that can be changed through reform and thus is of greater practical significance.
3. The decision-process course covered a broad range of material, with a primary focus on constitutional and administrative law. The course was to provide the student with a foundation for making sense out of the other classes by focusing on legal procedure, legal concepts, and analytical skills. Unlike the other courses, it was taught in lecture format.
4. For an empirical report of first-year Yale law students' reactions to the Socratic method, see Robert Stevens, "Law Schools and Law Students," *Virginia Law Review* 59 (1973): 638–51. For one of the more severe critiques of the method, see Duncan Kennedy, "How the Law School Fails: A Polemic," *Yale Review of Law and Social Action* 1 (Spring, 1970): 72–73.
5. According to figures compiled by the law school, 64% of the first-year students in fall, 1977, were from outside Colorado, but this figure included at least some students who had resided in the Denver area for some time prior to 1977. Seventy-six percent of the students in my sample were not married at the beginning of their law school careers.
6. For comparative data on first-year workloads at other law schools, see American Bar Association, Special Committee for the Study of Legal Education, *Law Schools and Professional Education* (Chicago: American Bar Association, 1980), pp. 39–40 (summarizing Pipkin's work in progress based on time diaries kept by a sample of nearly twelve hundred students from seven law schools); Edward L.

Kimball, Larry C. Farmer, and D. Glad Monse, "Ability, Effort and Performance among First-Year Law Students at Brigham Young University," *American Bar Foundation Research Journal* 1981 (1981): 676–77; Stevens, "Law Schools and Law Students," 652–55; and Guy R. Loftman, "Study Habits and Their Effectiveness in Legal Education," *Journal of Legal Education* 27 (1975): 418–72.

7. Howard S. Becker, Blanche Geer, Everett C. Hughes, and Anselm L. Strauss, *Boys in White: Student Culture in Medical School* (Chicago: University of Chicago Press, 1961). See chapters 5–10 for the authors' analysis of the first year of medical school.
8. My analysis of the first year focused on the first two quarters of law school. In turning immediately to the second and third years, I largely ignore the third quarter of the first year. Thus a brief comment is in order. In the third quarter, the anxiety of the first year fell significantly for many students. With contracts and torts, the two high-pressure courses behind them, many third-quarter students felt new confidence in their ability to succeed (although the posting of second-quarter grades was not completed until early May, about two-thirds of the way through the third quarter). In many ways, the third quarter was a transition period between the first and second years, blending the features of the first two quarters with the attributes of the second and third years.
9. Ronald M. Pipkin, "Legal Education: The Consumer's Perspective," *American Bar Foundation Research Journal* 1976 (1976): 1161–92; Robert Stevens, "Law Schools and Law Students," *Virginia Law Review* 59 (1973): 652–55; Guy R. Loftman, "Study Habits and Their Effectiveness in Legal Education," *Journal of Legal Education* 27 (1975): 418–72.
10. In studies based on data gathered at several law schools, both Stevens and Pipkin found behavior patterns for second- and third-year law students similar to those reported here (ibid.). In a more impressionistically based article, Bergin argues, "To be mercifully brief, law school is unmercifully dull because the only skill learned after the first year is the skill of feigning preparedness for class." Thomas F. Bergin, Jr., "The Law Teacher: A Man Divided against Himself," *Virginia Law Review* 54 (1968): 648.
11. Sharon's third interview indicated that between the second and third interviews she had shifted all the way to a preference for big-firm corporate work and then back to small-firm general practice.
12. American Bar Association, *Model Code of Professional Responsibility*, Ethical Consideration 2–25. A similar admonition appears as Rule 6.1 of the *Model Rules of Professional Conduct*, adopted by the ABA in 1983 as the successor to the Model Code.
13. I can only speak with certainty on these matters with regard to the courses I took. Of those courses, I have a nearly complete knowledge, having in three years missed only one class period that was not

tape-recorded for me by another student. I attended every meeting of my course on the legal profession. My guess is that the sections of the legal profession course taught by another professor—one whom Jenny Landis reported spent time on public interest concerns in his class on creditor-debtor relations—probably devoted more attention to the profession's obligation to serve the disadvantaged.

14. Robert Stevens, *Law School: Legal Education in America from the 1850s to the 1980s* (Chapel Hill: University of North Carolina Press, 1983), chap. 4.
15. For a systematic consideration of law student responses to curricular reform moving beyond the scope of traditional legal education, see Ronald M. Pipkin, "Law School Instruction in Professional Responsibility: A Curricular Paradox," *American Bar Foundation Research Journal* 1979 (1979): 247–75; and Pipkin, "Student Responses to Law School Curricula."
16. The questionnaire asked each student to provide information about his or her most recent (or contemporaneously held) legal job. Those who had held two or more jobs also provided information describing their second most recent job; and those who had held three or more jobs also described their third most recent job. This method produced 198 descriptions of legal jobs held outside the law school, 194 of which were complete enough to allow classification of the job.
17. The question referred to "law-related *jobs*" (emphasis added) and was intended to elicit responses concerning *paid* employment. However, a few of the "jobs" listed and described in the students' answers to the question were in fact academically sponsored student internships (up to six hours of course credit per quarter) or externships (fifteen hours of credit for a quarter of full-time work and a research paper). Externs working outside of Colorado sometimes received a living allowance, but neither externs nor interns were allowed to receive wages as such. I included these "jobs" in my tally on the theory that the respondents would not have designated them as such had they not involved activity essentially similar to paid employment by the organization in question. The overwhelming majority of the 194 jobs listed appeared to be paid positions. In contrast, a sizable proportion of the 21 public interest jobs listed appeared to be internships or externships. Information provided in the job descriptions themselves and in the students' answers to another question clearly implied that seven of these 21 jobs were of this type; extrapolating a bit and using additional clues within the student answers, it seems probable that half or more of the public interest jobs listed were academic internships or externships. In light of my decision to include these in my tally of jobs, it would have been desirable to make a definitive count of *all* internships and externships that were essentially similar to paid employment. Unfortunately, I did not explicitly inquire about this subject on my questionnaire. I did,

however, ask a more general question about public interest activities that should have elicited that information from those students who held internships or externships with a public interest organization. Using the answers to this question, I found three additional students who had held internships with public interest–oriented groups.

18. Edward O. Laumann and John P. Heinz, ''Specialization and Prestige in the Legal Profession,'' *American Bar Foundation Research Journal* 1977 (1977): 202, 204, 205. See also John P. Heinz and Edward O. Laumann, *Chicago Lawyers: The Social Structure of the Bar* (New York: Russell Sage Foundation; Chicago: American Bar Foundation, 1982).
19. Joel F. Handler, Ellen Jane Hollingsworth, Howard S. Erlanger, and Jack Ladinsky, ''The Public Interest Activities of Private Practice Lawyers,'' *American Bar Association Journal* 61 (Nov., 1975): 1388–94; see also Joel F. Handler, Ellen Jane Hollingsworth, and Howard S. Erlanger, *Lawyers and the Pursuit of Legal Rights* (New York: Academic Press, 1978), chap. 5.
20. Laumann and Heinz, 202.
21. I do not mean to imply that conventional law firms devote most of their efforts to representing greedy bankers against starving widows or land companies against environmentalists. Certainly they do not. Chapter 4 emphasizes that many students were surprised to discover just how benign conventional business practice was. But still, as the students quoted below point out, clerking for conventional firms did sometimes require students to work in opposition to their public interest values.
22. Leon Festinger, *A Theory of Cognitive Dissonance* (Stanford, Cal.: Stanford University Press, 1975).
23. For some data on the extent and consequences of student employment during law school, see Ronald M. Pipkin, ''Moonlighting in Law School: A Multischool Study of Part-Time Employment of Full-Time Students,'' *American Bar Foundation Research Journal* 1982 (1982): 1109–62, and Donald N. Zillman and Vickie R. Gregory, ''Law Student Employment and Legal Education,'' *Journal of Legal Education* 36 (1986): 390–402.

4 Reality and Myth

Sources of Changed Expectations about Law Jobs

Changes in Expectations of Craft Satisfaction

The young child smiled as she glanced up from her chair toward her mother, who was standing erect as she spoke a few feet away. The faces of both reflected the pleasure with which they worked. The daughter worked with crayons, creating bright images on white paper, enjoying a day's vacation from school. The mother worked with statutes, with appellate opinions, and with hypothetical fact situations, creating images of her own on the minds of the students in her course on the law of corporations. As she lectured she spoke with the intensity, authority, and precision that mark an excellent teacher. No concept was so complex that it couldn't be illuminated with an analogy or illustrated with an example. No student's question was too simple-minded to merit less than her full attention or so irrelevant that she could not subtly reshape it to the advantage of the entire class.

The child finished a picture and quietly interrupted her mother in midsentence. "Look, Mommy! Look at what I've made!" The mother's compliment took barely a second, but for that second her entire attention was directed to the child. Then with a smile to answer those on her students' faces, she returned to the fiduciary duty of a corporate officer.

I did not take any classes from this professor. I admit that my description of her sounds almost too good to be true. But more than one of the students I interviewed portrayed her in these terms. Barbara Phillips was in class the day the professor's daughter attended and later used the incident to help explain the influence that the professor had on her change in job preference to corporate law.

Barbara entered law school thinking that the intellectual content of corporate law would be boring and that "all corporate lawyers were white, upper-middle-class robber barons." The corporations class that she took as a second-year student exploded those myths and deeply altered her expectations concerning what it would be like to work for a large corporate law firm. The corporate lawyer who taught Barbara's class was a compassionate, personable woman whose life exemplified many of the goals that Barbara supported as a feminist. Furthermore, the professor taught corporate law in a way that challenged and stimulated Barbara's intellect more than any other course she had taken. By the end of the quarter, Barbara was hooked. Her plans for a feminist-oriented public interest practice dissolved, and she went on to take courses in securities regulation and compliance from her favorite professor before accepting a job in the corporate department of a top law firm.

I told Barbara's story in chapter 2, where I explained the shift in job preferences of students like her in terms of changes in their values and expectations. In chapter 3, I focused on changes in *values*, examining the source and influence of the values that tend to draw students away from a self-sacrificing commitment to public service. In this chapter I move on to analyze changes in *expectations* about the nature of different law jobs.

The statistical analysis in chapter 2 showed that three changes in expectations were of particular importance in accounting for the decrease in preference for jobs with public interest employers and the concomitant increase in preference for large and mid-sized firms, especially those involved in corporate law. First, declining expectations of long-term benefits—in particular, of valuable experience, knowledge, and professional contacts—were important factors behind the decreased preference for public interest jobs. Shifting expectations concerning the extent to which the jobs would allow the students to fulfill altruistic values contributed to the movement away from public interest jobs and toward work with medium-sized law firms specializing in business law. Finally, increased expectations of craft satisfaction contributed to an increased preference for corporate law.

This section of the chapter will examine the sources of the change in students' expectations about the opportunities for craft satisfaction in various jobs. I will argue that the changed perceptions of various jobs resulted from two types of new information. First, students acquired more accurate information about the legal world; the lay myths with which the students began were replaced by an expanding stock of experientially based knowledge. Second, some inaccurate information was replaced by other information that was also inaccurate, but which came from a different source; lay mythology was replaced by the mythology of the legal profession. The second part of the chapter will analyze the changes in expectations about the long-term benefits of different jobs and changes in expectations about the extent to which various jobs provide opportunities to serve altruistic goals.

"Sort of Like Playing Monopoly." Two shifts in perception appeared particularly important to the students' improved image of the amount of craft satisfaction to be found in business-oriented practice. First, as the students took business-oriented courses, they discovered that business law in general and corporate law in particular was far more intellectually and analytically challenging than they had imagined. The importance of this change was magnified by a growth in the students' appreciation for intellectual and analytical activities. Second, the students' experience both inside and outside the law school conveyed an equally appealing image of other aspects of corporate and business practice. Whereas at the outset many students conceived of the daily activities of the corporate lawyer as involving routine "paperwork," by the end of law school they were more likely to think of them in terms of the human drama involved in managing a large organization or pulling off a successful financial deal.

The importance of changing perceptions of the intellectual and analytical content of corporate and business law was illustrated by the comments of Barbara Phillips, Sharon Lollar, and Ellen Torgeson. Barbara's perception that only practice with a large corporate firm could provide the intellectually tough, "really brain-teasing challenge" that she desired was described in chapter 2. Sharon's and Ellen's reactions to the corporate law class similarly emphasized the intellectual challenge.

> [Before I took Corporations] I thought, 'I never want to get involved in this; I have no need for it.' I took it because it was a bar course and I figured I needed to know something about it. I'm finding it really challenging, or at least interesting. It's personally challenging because it's like little puzzles, little problems that you have to figure out. [Sharon]

> Before I took the course I thought it would probably be dull, but then when I started taking the course I realized it was very intricate, that there

> was a lot to deal with and it was a challenge for someone to work with it. . . . I think there's a lot of prestige and money in it, but it's hard. [Ellen]

The students' increasing appreciation for less cerebral attractions of corporate and business law was perhaps best captured by the classmate who told me that he had come to view corporate law as "sort of like playing Monopoly." For many students the allure of corporate law appeared to be less the opportunity to earn lots of money than the opportunity to play with lots of other people's money. Barbara Phillips explained during the middle of her second year that "you find the power really even more tempting than the money. . . . A year ago I think I never even would have considered taking a job with a corporate firm . . . and now I'm working as a clerk for primarily a corporate firm."

The influence of work experience on changes in perception was also illustrated by Will Goodman's description of his experience as a legal intern with a medium-sized corporation.

> That internship I did with the———corporation was interesting. It convinced me that I could actually probably do some kinds of corporate work where I thought before that was impossible. . . . I was in a situation where I could sit in on all the meetings, and I got what you might call a big picture—not only law, but management, day-to-day stuff, which was really fascinating. It's every bit as challenging as trial work or anything else—just dealing with all the regulations and the people, the organization, the management. It's all fascinating stuff. I may have found a new interest.

The basic course on corporations was taught both by the professor described at the beginning of this chapter and by an equally dynamic colleague who was the frequent recipient of law school teaching awards. But the students' enthusiasm for corporate law appears to have sprung not only from the charisma of these professors but also from the content of the courses. Although I took the basic corporations course from a third professor, I too felt a compelling attraction to the subject matter. The cases conveyed a sense of drama and conflict not present in most other courses. Despite my best intentions to the contrary, the materials stimulated a yearning to wheel and deal in the marketplace of American capitalism.

These favorable images of business practice seem to have been reinforced by messages from a variety of additional sources within the legal community. The dominant professional view of corporate practice places it at the pinnacle of creative and challenging legal practice.

For example, in Laumann and Heinz's study of the Chicago bar, a panel of experts rated tax law, antitrust law, and securities law as the most intellectually challenging of thirty specialties.[1] And the image of the corporate lawyer as manager of American capitalism appears to have been solidifying in the collective consciousness of the legal profession since at least the 1930s.[2]

Rising expectations of craft satisfaction from business-oriented practice were accompanied by decreased expectations of craft satisfaction from public interest practice. Thus by the fall of her second year, Jenny Landis's initially favorable perception of legal aid work had given way to the view that "it is more of a treadmill type of thing. You're just hit with cases and cases and cases." Similarly, Sharon Lollar had reevaluated the opportunities for intellectual stimulation presented by the altruistically oriented jobs to which she had formerly aspired. "I guess I feel that . . . the kind of practice I was interested in doing tends to get old real fast," she said.

The questionnaire data analyzed in Chapter 2 showed that, of the craft satisfaction aspects I asked about, only one—the deterioration of the belief that legal aid work would challenge one's ability—was significantly associated with a decline in preference for public interest jobs. But the interview and observational data suggest additional aspects not specifically addressed in the questionnaire. For example, Barbara Phillips's initial desire to work with a small group of feminist lawyers "for the advancement of women" faded as her perceptions of the intellectual and creative outlet provided by such work diminished. The extent of Barbara's shift in perception was illustrated at the end of her third year in law school, when she referred to her former dreams of feminist-oriented practice as no more than a previous desire "to do domestic relations" law. And that area of law, according to Barbara, is "basically boring" in "all kinds of ways." "I mean you *can* be creative" she explained, "but it seems to be that the legal parameters and even the social parameters of domestic relations are very limited."

The reasons for the declining expectations with regard to public interest practice are more difficult to identify than are those for the rising expectations for conventional business practice. Almost all students were exposed to a good deal of experiential data on the practice of business law through their course work and through their clerking jobs with conventional firms. Far fewer students took the course in poverty law, explored civil rights and liberties issues beyond the basic constitutional law course, served the poor by working in the Student Law Office, or clerked for public interest employers.[3]

Moreover, there are scattered indications that first-hand contact with public interest law may have helped lower, rather than raise, students' expectations concerning the craft satisfaction available in public interest practice. For example, Jenny Landis reported that her poverty law class was "a lot more laid back" than most courses and not really very challenging. And Nelson Fixx's description of his experience as an intern for the Environmental Protection Agency, which arguably is a public interest employer, shows his disillusionment with the degree of craft satisfaction to be found there.

> I quit because I didn't feel I was being productive. That was a big change—to be working in a position that should have been the real me, *should* have been. It was a prestigious position that paid well, and it was with a young, energetic agency. And it was boring. It was terribly boring. . . . [T]here were a lot of factors in this, but one was the agency itself, being a big federal bureaucracy, was pretty stifling. . . . It didn't seem like there was much being done to change the environment, to work on the expressed goals of the agency. Instead people were more concerned about the coffee breaks, about whose daughter was going out with who. A lot of gossip time. Very little work happened. Terrible support staff.

Overall, though, I do not believe that Jenny's and Nelson's reactions to their experience with public interest law were typical. Jenny's reaction was not shared by most other students enrolled in courses with a public interest emphasis. Louie Littell spoke enthusiastically of his poverty law course, and another one of my classmates told me that his poverty law professor made a special effort to present a stiff academic challenge. My limited interview data on the subject also suggest that students enrolled in advanced civil rights and civil liberties courses viewed the work as both stimulating and challenging.

More importantly, the questionnaire data suggest that students with public interest work experience were less likely than other students to move toward negative expectations of public interest jobs. For example, for the eighty students who did not work for any type of public interest organization during law school, there was a decrease in the expectation that a legal aid job would be challenging, while it appears that for students who worked in public interest jobs outside of legal aid, the decrease was less, and for the four students who worked in legal aid positions, the expectation that the new lawyer would find this work challenging actually appears to have increased (table 4.1). Because of the small number of students who worked in public interest jobs, these results must be viewed as tentative; however, similar patterns were found for each aspect of craft satisfaction for all public interest jobs for which data were collected.

Table 4.1 Work Experience and Changes in Expectation of Challenge in Legal Aid Work

Work Experience	Change in Mean Rating of Challenge in Legal Aid
No public interest job during law school (N = 80)	−.51**
Legal aid or services job during law school (N = 4)	+.25
Other public interest job during law school (N = 18)	−.22
Mean[a]	−.43**

Note: Table shows change in mean rating of likelihood that job in legal aid would "challenge your ability."

[a] See table 2.6.

** Statistically significant at the .05 level.

Thus most students who lowered their expectations of the amount of craft satisfaction to be found in public interest work did so not on the basis of firsthand experience, but rather appear to have relied primarily on secondhand impressions. Most practicing lawyers and law professors have no more firsthand experience with public interest practice than the typical law student, but a low evaluation of public interest law nevertheless seems firmly embedded in the legal profession's dominant belief patterns.[4] Lawyers commonly consider public interest practice in general, and legal aid work in particular, to be neither very challenging nor very creative. Lacking any substantial personal experience with public interest law, the average law student apparently moves toward this dominant point of view. Kennedy has pointed to the part played in this process of socialization by law faculties, who, he argues, convey the impression that legal aid work, "although morally exalted . . . is hopelessly dull and unchallenging."[5] My own observation was that the DU faculty played a much smaller role in the process than did the practicing bar.

Mythological and Nonmythological Change. There can be little doubt that changing expectations of craft satisfaction brought many students' perceptions of both conventional and public interest practice closer to reality. Corporate law is *not* just boring paper shuffling. Legal aid work *does* involve a large amount of tedious and routine work. It would be foolish to deny that most law students leave law school with a better understanding of the day-to-day reality of most jobs than they possessed three years earlier. Furthermore, much of this information is firmly grounded in either the student's own experience or in the scientifically verifiable experience of others.

But even taking all this for granted, we should not assume that students' perceptions of various jobs are free from the influence of deeply rooted subcultural myths of the legal community. The sine qua non of myth is not lack of factual accuracy but rather lack of empirical verification. Myths are widely held beliefs, typically socially cued rather than experientially based, which reduce anxiety or ambivalence among members of a particular culture or subculture. Myths conceal psychologically threatening perceptions or other potentially troubling discontinuities in belief systems. They help to solidify the myth-holder's valued role identities. Further, myths often support existing systems of stratification, legitimizing inequalities in power and privilege.[6]

The social scientist's understanding of myth is well conveyed by Edelman's discussion of the political mythology of mass publics.

> The themes a society emphasizes and re-emphasizes about its government may not accurately describe its politics; but they do at least tell us what men want to believe about themselves and their state. In some cultures men have chosen to believe that their rulers were gods or descendants of gods, or that they were divinely appointed to rule. Men have sometimes told themselves that the established machinery for selecting leaders and legislators necessarily produced rule by an able aristocracy, or rule in the interests of the chosen class: the proletariat, the warriors, or the large landholders. Often men have told themselves that their political institutions translate the will of people into public policies.
>
> In some metaphysical sense, all of these propositions may be true; but it is of more interest to the social scientist that they are often not demonstrable by scientific methods, that there are many exceptions to them, and that they continue to be believed in spite of the lack of evidence and the demonstrable exceptions. Clearly, beliefs like these serve functions other than the description of a country's political institutions. They help to hold men together and help to maintain an orderly state.[7]

Professional subcultures are not immune from similar mythologies. Thus it is worth asking whether the intellectual content of tax law, antitrust law, and securities law really sets those specialties as far apart from divorce law, personal injury law, and general family law (all rated at the bottom for intellectual challenge by Laumann and Heinz's panel) as the legal profession seems to believe. Or are the perceptions at least partly based on a mythology that supports existing divisions of power and privilege within the legal profession?

Kennedy contends that the conventional perceptions on these matters as communicated by professors to law students "are just nonsense—the rationalizations of law teachers who [yearn] upward, fear status degradation, and above all hate the idea of risk." He argues that "legal services practice, for example, is far more intellectually stimulating and demanding, even with a high case load, than most of what corporate lawyers do."[8]

One need not be quite so categorical to question the alleged disparity between the intellectual content of corporate specialties and other types of law. I, for one, did not find my courses in corporate and business subjects to be any more intellectually challenging than the others. And the analytical edifice on which the legal concepts for these subjects are built seemed to me no more elegant than those constructed in many other areas of law. But in a sense, all such arguments are futile because it is probably impossible to arrive at an objective standard of intellectual difficulty or elegance. The key question is not the accuracy of the beliefs; rather, it is the role they play in reducing ambivalence and in reinforcing valued self-identities and existing social relationships.

Consider, for example, Nelson Fixx's and Sharon Lollar's perceptions of corporate securities law. If the prospectus accompanying the issuance of a certain stock misrepresents or omits a material fact of concern to potential investors, the attorney who handled the legal work can be individually sued for the investors' losses—even if the mistake involved no negligence or fraudulent intent on the part of the attorney. Both Nelson and Sharon emphasized this point in describing the intellectual complexity of corporate law.

> [Securities law is a] highly specialized, very complicated area to which attaches, as we say in the legal profession, a lot of personal liability. In other words, if you make a bad decision as a corporate securities lawyer, you expose yourself to tremendous personal financial liability. People can take you to court and turn you into a pauper. There's big money in it. [Nelson]

> One thing I think is that there's a sort of strict liability under the federal statutes on securities so that if you violate a certain section you can be sued individually as a lawyer, so that's why I think the salaries are so high. [Sharon]

It is interesting that both Nelson and Sharon not only saw a relationship between the attorney's personal liability and the intellectual complexity or challenge of securities law, but also connected these factors to the prestige or economic rewards accruing to securities lawyers. Although much of the legal profession appears to accept the corporate securities lawyer's strict personal liability as evidence of intellectual ability and as a justification for high prestige and salary, the scientific foundation for the factual premise is weak. Very few securities lawyers ever actually suffer the penalties associated with personal liability. And while it is true that a moderate degree of intelligence is required to avoid material misrepresentations or omissions when issuing securities, a high tolerance for the tedium of endlessly gathering, sorting, summarizing, and checking factual information and assertions is probably more important than intellectual brilliance.

But again, my argument as to the facts is beside the point if Nelson's and Sharon's views were not empirically based but instead were socially cued responses to discontinuities in their own belief systems or self-images. Both Nelson and Sharon came to law school from backgrounds in serving the underprivileged, and both entered law school intending to pursue public interest careers. But by October of the second year both showed definite signs of rejecting public interest practice for more lucrative conventional careers. And both were clearly feeling a certain amount of anxiety about that change. For example, without interruption Sharon followed her explanation of the personal liability of the securities lawyer with the following comment: "I've even started to think in terms of, like, jobs that offer more salary, you know, and that sort of thing." Then, after a brief follow-up exchange with me, she continued: "OK, I've given up this emphasis on the clients, so why shouldn't I look at myself? I mean . . . if I felt like I really wanted to be helping people, I'd do it regardless of how much money I was making. I don't know. *I feel really funny saying this*" (emphasis added).

And Nelson followed up with this explanation of his growing uncertainty about his job preferences: "From what little I've seen, I don't want to just say at this point that I'll be working for the state or working for the Sierra Club, because I think a person who's environmentally conscious can do some good working for development companies, oil companies, coal companies. *I feel I should cut my tongue out for saying that*" (emphasis added).

Of course, it is impossible to know with certainty what, if any, psychological function was served by Nelson and Sharon's belief that strict personal liability explains the securities attorney's high level of rewards and illustrates the intellectual challenge of securities work. But the evidence presented so far is at least consistent with the possibility that their eagerness to accept these beliefs was in part a product of their need to justify their own movement toward conventional business practice. Both Nelson and Sharon were accustomed to conceiving of themselves as defenders of the downtrodden. But a year into law school, both had begun to reorient their thinking in directions that could lead them to serve primarily a business clientele. Thus we might expect them to be unusually receptive to beliefs that would justify their changing orientations and thereby reduce anxiety and ambivalence. Quick and uncritical acceptance of information presenting a favorable picture of conventional business practice or an unfavorable picture of public interest practice would ease the psychological adjustment.

My point is not that changing expectations about the craft satisfaction in various types of legal practice were entirely, or even primarily, based on myth. Rather, I simply wish to suggest that the psychological process of myth-building may have played *some* part in reinforcing and enlarging these changes.

Changes in Expectations of Opportunities for Long-Term Benefits and for Altruism

A law student was celebrating his birthday, and the guests were exuberant. In one corner of the room, two couples were throwing darts at a black and yellow target. A few feet away, three or four people sat on the floor experimenting with the effects of helium on the vocal cords, releasing gas into their mouths from brightly colored balloons, and then doubling up with laughter as they spoke to each other in hollow, high-pitched—and hardly lawyerlike—voices. Conversations around the room were animated. I was talking to a woman not in law school who was curious to learn what legal education was "really like." Attempting to impress her with my erudition, I mentioned that research at several schools had shown a decline during the law school years in students' desire for public interest practice. Overhearing my comment, a fellow law student leapt quickly into the conversation.

"So what?" he nearly shouted. "That doesn't prove anything! I don't have anything against public interest practice, but I want to work someplace where I'll get some decent training. At Legal Services, it's baptism by fire. Everybody's overworked. The quality of the practice is crummy! Lots of people just don't know that when they start law school. You can't ask people to make that kind of sacrifice!"

I was struck by the intensity of this man's concern, but not by the content of his remarks. Second- and third-year law students, I had learned, viewed the initial job after law school as a continuation of their legal training. They had little faith that law school could prepare them for the practical exigencies of legal practice, and they cared deeply about the experience, knowledge, and contacts that their first job would provide. Furthermore, during the course of their legal education they formed rather definite opinions about various employers in this regard. Large and medium-sized law firms generally were believed to be especially likely to provide new attorneys with a solid foundation of experience, knowledge, and contacts. Public interest employers were not. And as shown in chapter 2, substantial declines in the students' expectations for such career-related benefits from public interest practice contributed substantially to the aggregate drop in desire for such work.

In this section I will explore the reasons for this change in the students' perceptions of public interest law as a vehicle for "post-graduate" training. In addition, I will analyze similarly important changes in the students' expectations concerning the extent to which public interest jobs would allow them to achieve altruistic goals.

Long-Term Career Benefits. Why did the DU students lose confidence in the quality of experience, knowledge, and contacts to be found in public interest practice? Evidence from questionnaire responses, interviews, and my observations coalesce with a bit of reasoned conjecture to provide a tentative answer. The aggregate drop in expectations appears to have resulted from at least three distinct shifts in the students' image of public interest practice.

First, the students' perception of the resources commanded by public interest institutions appears to have declined as their earlier, media-based images of these jobs were replaced by more realistic pictures of limited budgets and heavy caseloads. For example, Sharon Lollar explained her disillusionment with the value of legal aid work as a source of additional training as follows: "I think they're really restricted as far as the time they can spend on cases—the caseloads are enormous, I think—and feeling like they don't have as good facilities as in a private firm." Similarly, Jenny Landis mentioned in explaining her disillusionment with public defender and legal aid work that "there's a lack of government resources. It's always going to be that way." Other students specifically contrasted the training available at the city's resource-rich larger law firms with the more limited opportunities in public interest practice.

Second, it seems likely that there was significant change in the students' judgments concerning the proximity of public interest law to the mainstream of legal practice. This shift in perceptions was probably especially important to students who initially thought of public interest jobs as way stations in careers that might later head in more conventional directions. As these students learned how few attorneys in fact are engaged in public interest practice, they may have worried that public interest jobs would not place them at or near the center of the informal networks helpful in building professional contacts. Similarly, as they learned how little interest some conventional law firms have in legal specialties associated with most public interest jobs, they might have concluded that a job with a minority rights organization, for example, would not provide widely marketable skills and knowledge. Anxiety about the long-term benefits of early public interest practice was probably heightened as students learned to differentiate between the skills and knowledge appropriate to various legal specialties. For example, a beginning law student might overestimate the similarity of public defender work to conventional business practice, but a third-year student probably would not.

Third, as their contacts with the legal profession increased, the students discovered the generally low repute in which many attorneys hold public interest practice. Recall Laumann and Heinz's finding that even with other factors held constant, Chicago lawyers rated those legal specialties with the highest reputation for altruism as the lowest in terms of professional prestige. My own experience is that members of conventional law firms frequently assume that some, if not all, public interest organizations are staffed by disproportionately large numbers of sloppy, marginally qualified lawyers—hardly the type of colleagues likely to create a professional environment from which a new attorney might draw valuable experience, knowledge, and contacts.

Some DU students appeared to adopt these attitudes as their own. For example, in response to a questionnaire item requesting an explanation of changes in job preferences during law school, a student wrote that working as a law clerk had exposed him to "the lesser quality of law in public interest settings there and the vastly reduced lateral mobility one would have from that base. At a larger firm, lateral mobility is maximized and 'training' (e.g., with exposure to many areas of law) is also maximized." Furthermore, students who recognized but did not adopt the views of their professional elders may also have lowered their estimates of the value of public interest practice. Regardless of one's own opinion on the subject, recognizing the professional bias against public interest practice could lead one to question the career benefits of early experience in a public interest job.

Opportunities to Work for Altruistic Goals. In chapter 2, I showed that declining preferences for four public interest jobs were linked with declining expectations that those jobs would satisfy altruistic values. At the same time, the rise in preferences for jobs with medium-sized law firms specializing in business law was associated with increasing expectations of opportunities for altruism in those jobs. Further analysis (reported in chapter 5) also supports the position that these changes were not primarily a product of changes in group sympathies or political ideology; instead, they appear to have involved shifts in the students' perceptions concerning the extent to which the jobs in question would allow an attorney to do public interest work.

It is only a slight exaggeration to say that some of the DU students began their legal studies with a caricatured image of business-oriented practice, in which attorneys with such firms pursued starving widows on behalf of avaricious creditors, defended rich, bigoted employers against race and sex discrimination suits, and represented real estate developers hell-bent on destroying the pristine beauty of the Colorado mountainside. Clerking for a conventional law firm exploded that myth, as students discovered that business law practice is far more benign. It is not that business lawyers are never involved in disputes such as those caricatured, but simply that any such activity is a much smaller part of most business law firms' practice than many students had assumed. And to the extent that the common activities of business law firms do contribute to the economic oppression of underprivileged groups, the methods are almost always more subtle.

In addition, the students' exposure to business practice led them to personalize their cognitive images of a business law firm's clientele. For example, a law clerk working on a legal problem for Smith Office Supply Co. would soon discover that the real client is a particular Ms. or Mr. Smith. The clerk might even meet the client and learn that he or she roots for the Cubs, drives a pale blue Buick, and graduated from Purdue. A surprisingly large number of the students I interviewed seemed genuinely surprised to discover that working for a small or medium-sized business law firm would allow them to help "ordinary" (upper-middle-class) people.[9]

For example, among the students I formally interviewed, Barbara Phillips and Ellen Torgeson were particularly influenced by such changes in perception. In the fall of her second year, Barbara explained that a good deal of her "previous prejudice against working for a corporate firm was not knowing what kind of law they do." But after working as a law clerk for an eight-attorney firm specializing in corporate law, she was surprised to discover that although some of the firm's clients were "pretty vile . . . for the most part they're not." Furthermore, she learned that

> a lot of what we do is take . . . two or three people doing some kind of business venture and make corporations out of them, as much for tax and legal purposes as anything else. But I don't think that makes corporations the bad seed. So I don't feel as bad about working there.

Ellen pointed to similar changes in her perceptions of business practice as one factor important to her increased willingness to pursue such a career.

> I can [now] see working with smaller businesses because I think it's valid if you want to get together with a friend and start up a business, end up with an exciting venture. And it's not like businessmen are this group of alien people.

In contrast, the students' disillusionment with the altruistic potential of public interest practice appears to have resulted from their reassessment of both the effectiveness of law as a tool for social change and the institutional capacity of public interest organizations. By the fall of her second year, Barbara Phillips had abandoned the belief that she could use her position as an attorney to work effectively for her left-wing political goals. During one short segment of an interview, she made these statements.

> I don't think the law is particularly a tool for change. . . . I don't see being an attorney as being an expression of my politics; it's something I'll be good at. . . . Nothing I do as an attorney will cause radical change.

A number of students began to question whether particular public interest employers possessed the resources, institutional commitment, or organizational structure necessary to accomplish their goals. Barbara Phillips, Sharon Lollar, and Jenny Landis all made the point that heavy caseloads and limited resources severely limited the ability of legal aid attorneys to adequately represent indigent clients. Again in Barbara's words,

> I'm not sure if I recognize the validity of the whole legal services structure. I have some doubts about that. . . . It's just become a mill that you run people through, and some of the problems they handle, and some of them they don't. . . . A lot of that has to do with workload.

After internships with the Environmental Protection Agency, both Nelson Fixx and Ellen Torgeson expressed doubts about the capacity of that agency to truly protect the environment. Nelson's analysis of the problem was directed toward what might be summarized as bureaucratic inefficiency. Ellen's concerns were less clearly articulated.

The Mythological Element. Many of the shifts I have just described resulted from the confrontation of myth with empirical reality. Unseemly caricatures of business practice were replaced by the duller but more comfortable reality of lawyers serving ordinary, upper-middle-class people. Glittery images of public interest practice gave way to the realization of limited budgets and heavy caseloads, and students lowered their expectations of career benefits and altruistic potential accordingly. But as I argued with respect to expectations of craft satisfaction, one should also consider the possibility that some lay mythology was replaced not by fact but by the mythology of the legal profession.

Consider the case of Ellen Torgeson. As Ellen became more pessimistic about the opportunities to help the environment as an attorney for the Environmental Protection Agency, she became more optimistic about the opportunities to do so as a natural resources attorney for a conventional law firm or business corporation. According to Ellen, the advantage of business-oriented practice was that it would provide a more direct opportunity for her to convince businesses to adopt environmentally enlightened policies. It is clear that the emergence of this view was in part the product of an unusual receptiveness to "good news" about business-oriented practice. In Ellen's own words,

> I'm trying to open my mind towards working for corporations because there's a lot of jobs there for, well, natural resources law in a corporation, and it would be a good place to get experience. But it wouldn't be corporate law.

By accepting the view that business-oriented practice would allow her to work for the goal of environmental protection, Ellen appears to have been protecting her self-image as a strong environmentalist and shielding herself from the anxiety and guilt that might have resulted from simply abandoning environmentalist goals. If this interpretation is correct, Ellen's newly formed perception of business-oriented practice (and perhaps also her changing image of the Environmental Protection Agency) was in part mythical.

Students who for any number of reasons found themselves turning away from public interest practice probably reacted in a manner similar to Ellen's, easing and reinforcing this change in job preference through the psychological process of myth formation. The point is not that these shifts in perception were totally unrelated to reality. Public interest resources are indeed limited, and public interest law is less proximate to the mainstream of legal practice than many first-year law students believe. But there is more to it than this. I believe that the facts are exaggerated into myth—mostly unconsciously—by lawyers and students who seek to rationalize their own failure to support public interest efforts, who hope to shine through comparison of their job to public interest work or who seek to legitimize their position of privilege within the profession.

Conclusion

This chapter has attempted to explain the movement toward more negative expectations for public interest jobs and more positive expectations for conventional, business-oriented jobs. These shifts appear to have been the product of two sorts of learning processes. First, lay mythology was replaced by more accurate, experientially based perceptions of both sorts of practice. Second, to some extent lay mythology was replaced by the mythology of the legal profession.

At DU I saw little evidence that either law professors themselves, or the written material which they assigned, directly conveyed a negative image of the craft satisfaction, long-term benefits, or opportunities for altruistic action available from public interest practice. Instead, students appeared to be more frequently exposed to such sentiments by practicing attorneys or by fellow law students who themselves had acquired their views from practicing lawyers. Thus the law school seems to play a much less important role than the practicing bar in transmitting the professional myth of public interest ineptitude and marginality.

However, it would be incorrect to conclude that the law school's stance toward public interest practice was irrelevant to the students' changing expectations. Viewed from one perspective, this stance might be characterized as demand-responsive neglect: the law school would increase its meager public interest emphasis if student demand justified it. But in the meantime, students learned very little about public interest practice unless they made special efforts to interact with the small number of professors, courses, or student organizations likely to provide the relevant information. In contrast, they learned a great deal about conventional business practice, unless they made deliberate efforts to avoid the profusion of information on that subject.

NOTES

1. Edward O. Laumann and John P. Heinz, "Specialization and Prestige in the Legal Profession: The Structure of Deference," *American Bar*

Foundation Research Journal 1977 (1977): 155–216 (see table 1, p. 167). See also John P. Heinz and Edward O. Laumann, *Chicago Lawyers: The Structure of the Bar* (New York: Russell Saga Foundation; Chicago: American Bar Foundation, 1982).

2. For example, see Samuel Untermyer, "What Every Present-Day Lawyer Should Know," *The Annals of the American Academy of Political and Social Sciences* 167 (May, 1933): 173–74.
3. More detailed data on the number of students exposed to public interest work experiences and to the Student Law Office appear in chapter 6.
4. As reported in chapter 2, Laumann and Heinz found that even with other factors held constant, Chicago lawyers rated those legal specialties with the highest reputations for altruism the lowest on prestige. Laumann and Heinz, "Specialization and Prestige," 202; see also Heinz and Laumann, *Chicago Lawyers.*
5. Duncan Kennedy, "Legal Education as Training for Hierarchy," in David Kairys, ed., *The Politics of Law: A Progressive Critique* (New York: Pantheon Books, 1982), p. 51.
6. This description of myth is drawn primarily from the various writings of Murray Edelman, including particularly *The Symbolic Uses of Politics* (Urbana: University of Illinois Press, 1964), *Politics as Symbolic Action* (Chicago: Markham Press, 1971), and *Political Language: Words that Succeed and Policies that Fail* (New York: Academic Press, 1977).
7. Edelman, *The Symbolic Uses of Politics*, pp. 191–92.
8. Kennedy, p. 52.
9. In some sense these changes resulted in the students' developing a more favorable image of business, as is suggested by the statements of Barbara Phillips and Ellen Torgeson. In addition, analysis of the questionnaire data showed that 18% of the variance in changes in expectations that "working for a medium-sized business law firm would allow one to help persons or groups with whom he identifies or sympathizes" was explained by questions measuring changes in group sympathies.

5 Growing Older, Turning Right, In Need of a Job

Some Alternative Explanations of Changed Job Preferences

I speared twin melon balls on my toothpick, ate one, and deposited the other beside the raspberry pastry on the small plate in my left hand. Then I headed for the champagne table. The large room, lined with tables full of delicacies, was packed with newly anointed lawyers and their families and friends. Earlier in the afternoon, we had been inducted to the bar. Now we were celebrating at a reception hosted by the Colorado Bar Association, eagerly congratulating each other, reminiscing, and trading job descriptions.

As I looked around the room, I was suddenly struck by what seemed an amazing phenomenon: my classmates actually looked like lawyers. Three years before, I had noticed that many of them were barely distinguishable from the undergraduate students I taught. As entering law students, 59 of the 103 questionnaire respondents had been twenty-three years old or younger. But three years seemed to have transformed even the youngest into adult professionals. Nobody could mistake this for a room full of undergraduates. The difference between a twenty-two-year-old beginning law student and a twenty-five-year-old attorney was immense.

One explanation for this transformation is that through a subtle process of professional socialization law students learn to carry themselves like attorneys, as they learn to think of themselves as attorneys. But a far simpler explanation is that the changes I noted were primarily the product of physical maturation resulting from the simple passage of time. Might not something similar account for the shifts in job preferences?

Thus far, I have explained changes in job preferences by emphasizing the importance of values and expectations related to public interest jobs. This chapter will consider three competing explanations. The first of these alternative explanations is that the DU law students' drift away from public interest law was at least in part the product of a loss of idealism which frequently occurs as people grow older, particularly when they face the demands of independent economic survival. The second alternative is that the change in job preferences reflects changes in the students' broader political ideology, brought on by the law school socialization process or by broader political changes in society. Finally, I will consider whether the loss of desire for public interest practice was primarily a response to an employment market that provided too few job opportunities in public interest law.

"Growing Older"

Determining the extent to which aging accounted for shifts in the students' job preferences is not easy. The obvious strategy—comparing DU law students to a control group of non–law students of the same age—would not work, because measuring non–law students' preferences for legal jobs would be meaningless. Thus it is necessary to approach the issue indirectly.

If the drift away from public interest law resulted from some aspect of the students' getting older, then we would expect to find a negative relationship between age and preference for public interest practice at any given point in time. That is, at both the beginning and the end of law school we would expect younger students to have stronger preferences than older students for public interest law, and older students to have stronger preferences for conventional jobs. The result would be the same if the drift away from public interest law were the result of the "conservative" impact of impending economic independence; older students are more likely to support themselves than are younger students and thus, even at the beginning of law school, would be more likely than younger students to have already experienced a shift in job preferences. On the other hand, if aspects of aging are not important causes of changes in job preferences, then we would expect to find little relationship between age and job preferences at any single point in time.

Data from the questionnaire indicate that there is no substantial relationship either at Time 1 or Time 2 between age and the students' ratings of the various jobs (table 5.1). Moreover, whatever relationship exists is in the opposite direction of that predicted by an explanation

Table 5.1 Correlation between Age and Job Preferences

Job Preference	Time 1	Time 2
Public Interest Jobs		
ACLU staff attorney	.07	.03
Legal aid or services	.09	.11*
Minority rights group	.09	.07
Public defender	.06	.09
Public interest law center	.06	.08
Public interest lobby	.13*	−.02
Small firm—much public interest	.02	.02
Business-oriented private firms		
Large firm, corporate law	−.08	−.04
Medium firm, business law	−.09	−.02
Small firm, business law	−.09	−.06
Other private firms		
Medium firm, general	−.15*	−.02
Small firm, litigation	−.14*	−.13*
Small firm, general	.01	−.05

Note: Table shows correlation between age and preference for job listed, as measured by Kendall's Tau. N for each coefficient varies between 101 and 103.

* Statistically significant at .15 level.

attributing the abandonment of public interest law to aspects of "getting older."[1] In general, older students are more likely than other students to be interested in public interest jobs and less interested in conventional jobs, but none of the relationships is statistically significant at the .05 level. A separate analysis of the possibility that *change* in job preference was related to age led to similar results. For example, focusing on those thirty-eight students who expressed some preference for public interest practice when they entered law school, I found the correlation between age and the retention of that preference at graduation to be .02 as measured by Kendall's Tau. In sum, these data do not support an interpretation that attributes the drift away from public interest law to factors related to aging.

Changes in Political Beliefs

Some observers of legal education have argued that the drift away from public interest practice during law school is accounted for by socialization to conservative belief systems and to conventional conceptions of the attorney's proper role. Critics of legal education writing in the late 1960s and early 1970s were especially likely to suggest such explanations. Green and Van Loon, for example, write that law school lowers the attractiveness of public interest practice by making students more politically conservative.[2] Savoy argues that law school generates a shift toward social conservatism, producing "predictable people who will be placidly assimilated in the Bar Association."[3] And many critics contend that a pro-business orientation pervades most law schools, so that over time students adopt more favorable attitudes toward business and less favorable attitudes toward antibusiness interests or disadvantaged groups.[4]

Other observers have argued that during law school students modify their conception of the lawyer's proper professional role in ways that discourage public interest practice. First, according to this view, law school teaches that a lawyer can best advance the public interest through willing advocacy of any position, regardless of its political or social consequences.[5] The claimed result is that new attorneys, whatever their political ideology, are willing to offer their services to the highest bidder. Second, legal training is said to encourage law students to see the lawyer's role in terms of a narrow, technical, legalistic expertise that precludes concern with broad social and political issues.[6] Third, proponents of this view assert that legal training discourages public interest work by imparting the belief that a lawyer should be concerned with protecting the interest of individual clients to the exclusion of trying to reform or improve society.[7] Finally, it is said that even those students steadfastly committed to using the law for overtly political ends often redefine the lawyer's role so as to reject the potentially effective political means of using litigation for political mobilization and organization.[8] The tactics of a Ralph Nader or a William Kunstler are discarded for more conventional modes of legal activity.

Moreover, quite apart from any changes in political identification or professional attitude that are generated through the law school experience, the job preferences of the DU students might have changed as a reflection of broader societal trends in public opinion and political culture. A good deal of folk wisdom points to two relevant national trends. First, the years between 1976 and 1980 might be seen as a crucial period during which the mood of public opinion shifted significantly in a conservative direction. Ronald Reagan's convincing electoral victory in 1980 seems to support such a view. Given that the type of public interest law I focused on is linked to political liberalism, a shift to a more conservative ideology might have helped account for the changes in job preferences. Second, whereas the late 1960s are commonly described as a period of political and social activism, public attitudes are often said to have shifted throughout the 1970s toward the more materialistic and self-centered concerns of a "me generation." Furthermore, this trend is sometimes identified as having occurred most markedly on the college campuses, where it presumably would have affected the career preferences of law students.

Tables 5.2 through 5.5 report the responses of the DU students to a number of questions used to examine these explanations. First, students were asked to classify their political ideology in terms of the categories listed in table 5.2. Comparing their Time 1 and Time 2 responses, we can see a drift towards conservativism. The number of students who categorized themselves as very liberal or radical dropped from 20 to 13 (although the number of self-proclaimed radicals actually increased by 1), while the number of conservative and very conservative students increased from 16 to 19.

The concept of social conservatism is not easy to operationalize, but the students were asked two questions intended to serve as indicators of the sort of social conservatism that Savoy argues would lead to "placid assimilation" into the bar association.[9] The small changes in the mean responses to both questions were in the direction of increased social conservatism, but were not statistically significant (table 5.3).

Table 5.4 reports the students' level of agreement with several items designed to gauge their support for various political interests. On all

Table 5.2 Self-Characterized Political Ideology

	Number at Time 1	Number at Time 2	Change
(1) Very conservative	0	2	+2
(2) Conservative	16	17	+1
(3) Moderate	35	36	+1
(4) Liberal	31	31	0
(5) Very liberal	16	8	−8
(6) Radical	4	5	+1
No answer	1	4	+3
Total	103	103	
Mean	3.59	3.41	−.18**

Note: Table shows frequency of self-characterization into categories listed. N = 103.
** Change in mean is statistically significant at the .05 level.

Table 5.3 Social Conservatism

	Mean at Time 1	Mean at Time 2	Change[a]
As an attorney, I would enjoy having a reputation among fellow members of the bar as being somewhat nonconformist.	3.33	3.24	−.09
It is important that individual attorneys protect the public image of the legal profession by refraining from bizarre or unconventional behavior	2.79	2.96	+.17

Note: Mean on five-point scale; score of five indicates strong agreement with statement.
[a] Neither difference was statistically significant at the .15 level.

three items measuring support for business interests, the students' mean level of support increased at least slightly. Of these three items, the greatest increase was for the statement "More should be done to protect the economic and property rights of business against government regulation and control." For this item, the mean level of agreement increased .32 on a five-point scale, reflecting the fact that the number of respondents who agreed or strongly agreed with the statement rose from 35 to 55.

The level of agreement with items measuring support for anti-business interests decreased .27 for "More should be done to protect the position of the consumer relative to that of businesses that produce and distribute goods and services" and decreased .38 for "More should be done to protect the environment against abuses by big business and others." The number of respondents who strongly agreed dropped from 44 to 25 for the first of these items and from 63 to 46 for the second.

The remainder of the data shows small declines in agreement with statements measuring support for the poor, racial minorities, and "basic civil rights and civil liberties" (table 5.4). Thus the main change that occurred in the students' evaluation of various group interests was an increase in support for business interests, especially with regard to protection against government regulation and control, and a drop in support for the consumer and environmental interests challenging business. Nonetheless, the mean ratings for the items critical of business interests remain higher than those supporting business.

Table 5.5 summarizes the law students' responses to questions on those aspects of role identity thought to discourage public interest

Table 5.4 Support for Various Political Interests

	Mean at Time 1	Mean at Time 2	Change
Business interests			
More should be done to protect the economic and property rights of business against government regulation and control.	3.04	3.36	+.32**
It is important that big business continue to play a major role in the American system.	3.48	3.62	+.14
More should be done to protect the interests of business against the challenge posed by activists claiming to represent environmental and consumer concerns.	2.47	2.51	+.04
Interests challenging business			
More should be done to protect the position of the consumer relative to that of businesses that produce and distribute goods and services.	4.11	3.84	−.27
More should be done to protect the environment against abuses by big business and others.	4.51	4.13	−.38**
Other interests			
More should be done to improve the economic and social position of blacks, Chicanos, Native Americans, and other racial minorities.	3.97	3.86	−.11
More should be done to provide for the needs of persons living below or close to the poverty level.	4.02	3.88	−.14*
More should be done to protect the economic and social position of the middle class.	3.35	3.38	+.03
More should be done to protect basic civil rights and civil liberties such as freedom of speech, press, and religion, and the rights of persons espousing unpopular views.	4.11	4.05	−.06

Note: Mean on five-point scale; score of five indicates strong agreement with statement.

* Statistically significant at .15 level.

** Statistically significant at .05 level.

Table 5.5 Professional Role Orientation

	Mean at Time 1	Mean at Time 2	Change
Lawyers should be more concerned with solving technical legal problems than with solving broader political and social problems.	2.11	2.32	+.21**
A lawyer should be more concerned with protecting the interests of his individual clients than with trying to reform the law to improve society.	2.84	3.28	+.44**
The distinctive skills of the legal profession include ability in activities such as lobbying, investigative research, political organizing, and public relations.	3.36	3.36	0

Note: Mean on five-point scale; score of five indicates strong agreement with statement.
** Statistically significant at .05 level.

practice. The first item in the table measures agreement with the idea that "lawyers should be more concerned with solving technical legal problems than with solving broader political and social problems." Support for this view rose by .21. Whereas at the beginning of law school only five of the students agreed or strongly agreed with the statement, by their final quarter in law school, 17 did. The next item, which asked whether "a lawyer should be more concerned with protecting the interests of his individual clients than with trying to reform the law to improve society," showed the greatest change. The mean level of agreement increased by .44, with those agreeing and strongly agreeing nearly doubling from 28 to 51. Finally, the data for the third item in the table fail to support the hypothesis that law school socializes students to reject more effective modes of political action in favor of a conventional litigation strategy. There was no change in the mean level of agreement with "The distinctive skills of the legal profession include ability in activities such as lobbying, investigative research, political organizing, and public relations."

Of the fifteen items in tables 5.2 through 5.5, there are only six for which aggregate change was statistically significant at the .05 level, and one additional item at the .15 level. And even for these, we must still ask whether those changes are associated with changes in job preferences at the *individual* level—that is, are the students who arguably

Table 5.6 Changes in Job Preferences Explained by Changes in Political Ideology, Professional Role Conceptions, and Relevant Group Sympathies

Change in Preference for:	Variance Explained
Legal aid or services	.12
Public defender	.13
Minority rights organization	.15
Public interest law center	.05
Medium firm, business law	.14
Large firm, corporate law	.09

Note: Table shows squared multiple-partial correlation coefficients, controlling for Time 1 values.

became more conservative the same ones who report a reduced preference for public interest jobs? To examine this question, various subsets of the six variables were used in a series of regression analyses where the dependent variable was change in job preference. Each of these regressions included the following independent variables: (1) change in self-defined political ideology, (2) change in the two measures of professional role orientation, and (3) change in the group sympathy items most relevant to the job preference in question—for example, the items on support for consumers and support for the poor were included when the dependent variable was preference for legal aid or services work.

The individual-level relationships between these independent variables and changes in job preferences were not strong. The six regression analyses summarized in table 5.6 are illustrative of twenty regressions analyzed. The coefficients in the table assess the extent to which the independent variables explain the variance in the dependent variables—the changes in job preferences.[10] In each of the six analyses, the variance explained is .15 or less.[11] Thus, while changes in political self-identification, group sympathies, and professional role orientations do occur during law school, they appear to have only a limited (although not necessarily inconsequential) impact on aggregate changes in job preferences.[12]

The Influence of the Job Market

Erlanger and Klegon have suggested that information about the job market may act to shape students' orientations toward public interest practice,[13] possibly causing students to turn away from public interest law as they increasingly come to perceive that the demand for public interest lawyers is limited. Students concerned about their employability in public interest jobs may try to prepare for alternative careers and may be influenced by psychological and sociological forces having the potential to affect job preferences. For one thing, these students may steel themselves against future disappointment by adjusting their preferences to conform to reality as they perceive it. In addition, preparing for the contingencies of an uncertain job market may expose students to environments particularly unsupportive of public interest practice. An obvious example would be a student who takes business law courses and accepts a student clerkship with a business law firm. However, the decline in preference for public interest practice cannot be attributed to the students' changing perceptions of the market for public interest attorneys unless (1) there was an aggregate drop in the students' confidence concerning their chances for public interest job offers, and (2) individual students who lost that confidence actually ended up with a reduced preference for public interest jobs. Both of these issues can be addressed with the data gathered for the DU students.

Table 5.7 reports mean changes in perceived employability in various jobs. The data are based on the students' responses to a question which asked them to assume that they had applied for each job and to rate their chance of receiving a job offer as "very good," "fairly good," or "not very good." Respondents were also permitted to state that they "lacked sufficient information" to assess their changes. Responses of "very good" were given a score of three; "fairly good" and "lack of sufficient information" were given a two; and answers of "not very good" were given a one.

The data indicate that over time the students became less optimistic about their ability to obtain public interest jobs. This shift in perception was particularly great for jobs with a public defender office and with a public interest lobbying group. Data not shown in the table show that the number of students rating their chances for a public defender job as "not very good" rose from 16 to 29 between the beginning and the end of law school; for a job with a public interest lobby group, the increase was from 16 to 27.

At the same time, the data show an *increase* in the students' perceived employability with small and medium-sized general practice firms and with small firms specializing in criminal and personal injury litigation. This pattern does not hold, however, for private law firms specializing in business law. Here, just as for public interest jobs, the students became more pessimistic about their employment chances. The shift was especially great for work with large firms specializing in

Table 5.7 Perceived Employability for Various Jobs

	Mean at Time 1	Mean at Time 2	Change
Public interest jobs			
ACLU staff attorney	1.88	1.82	−.06
Legal aid or services	2.27	2.14	−.13*
Minority rights organization	1.85	1.73	−.12*
Public defender	2.13	1.92	−.21**
Public interest law center	2.07	1.95	−.12*
Public interest lobby	2.17	1.96	−.21**
Small firm—much public interest	2.08	2.19	+.11
Business-oriented private firms			
Large firm, corporate law	1.78	1.62	−.16*
Medium firm, business law	1.99	1.93	−.06
Small firm, business law	2.05	2.03	−.02
Other private firms			
Medium firm, general	2.06	2.18	+.12*
Small firm, litigation	2.01	2.13	+.12
Small firm, general	2.22	2.41	+.19**

Note: Mean on three-point scale; score of three indicates very good chance of receiving an offer if respondent applied for this job; two indicates fairly good chance or lack of sufficient information to assess; one indicates not a very good chance.

* Statistically significant at .15 level.

** Statistically significant at .05 level.

corporate law. The number of students rating their chances for such a job as "not very good" rose from 38 to 55 between the beginning and the end of law school. This shift is particularly interesting because, as reported in chapter 2, the number of students hoping to work for large corporate firms increased substantially over time.

Table 5.8 shows the results of regression analyses which assessed the extent to which change in preference for each job listed is affected by change in the perceived chance of successfully competing for that job. Each line in the table is based on a regression analysis in which the dependent variable was the change in preference for the job listed (e.g. ACLU staff attorney), and the independent variable was the change in perceived employability for that job, controlling for the Time 1 levels of job preference and perceived employability in the job. The table shows the standardized regression coefficient for the independent variable in each of the six analyses; in addition, to facilitate comparison to analyses presented earlier, an estimate of the variance explained

Table 5.8 Changes in Job Preference Explained by Changes in Perceived Employability

Change in preference for:	Standardized Regression Coefficient	Estimated Variance Explained
ACLU staff attorney	.13	.02
Legal aid or services	.14*	.02
Minority rights organization	.19**	.04
Public defender	.38**	.14
Public interest law center	.10	.01
Public interest lobby	.32**	.10

Note: Table shows results of regression analysis, controlling for Time 1 values.
* Statistically significant at the .15 level.
** Statistically significant at the .05 level.

by that variable is shown.[14] While the effect of changes in perceived employability is statistically significant at the .05 level for three jobs (work with a minority rights organization, work with the public defender, and work with a public interest lobbying group), in all cases the change in perceived employability explains less than 15% of the variance.[15]

Conclusion

In the previous chapters, I focused on the effect which the law school experience—broadly conceived so as to include contact with the practicing bar—has on the job preferences of law students. The present chapter, in contrast, has explored three alternative explanations for the shift away from public interest jobs: (1) aging, maturation, or related processes, (2) a shift in political orientation and related professional role orientations, and (3) students' declining confidence in the market for public interest attorneys. While these alternatives have merit, the explanation set forth in the preceding chapters—focusing on changes in values and in expectations about the ability of various jobs to fulfill those values—remains viable.

NOTES

1. Similarly, the relationship between age and responses to the open-ended question on job preference was negligible and in the opposite direction of that predicted by the "aging" explanation.

2. Mark J. Green, "The Young Lawyers, 1972: Goodbye to Pro Bono," *New York Magazine* 5 (February 21, 1972): 29, 32. Eric E. Van Loon, "The Law School Response: How to Sharpen Students' Minds by Making Them Narrow," in Bruce Wasserstein and Mark J. Green, eds., *With Justice for Some* (Boston: Beacon Press, 1970), p. 338.
3. Paul N. Savoy, "Toward a New Politics of Legal Education," *Yale Law Journal* 79 (1970): 460.
4. For example, Van Loon, p. 337; Erwin N. Griswold, "The Intellect and Spirit" in Arthur E. Sutherland, ed., *The Path of the Law from 1967* (Cambridge, Mass.: Harvard University Press, 1968), p. 151;. David N. Rockwell, "The Education of the Capitalist Lawyer: The Law School," in Robert Lefcourt, ed., *Law against the People* (New York: Vintage, 1971), pp. 90–104; Ralph Nader, "Law School and Law Firms," *Minnesota Law Review* 43 (1970): 493–501.
5. Stuart Scheingold, *The Politics of Rights* (New Haven: Yale University Press, 1974), pp. 162–69, especially p. 166; Van Loon.
6. Scheingold, p. 162; Nader, p. 493; Griswold, p. 149; Abraham S. Goldstein, "The Unfulfilled Promise of Legal Education," in Geoffrey C. Hazard, ed., *Law in Changing America* (New York: American Assembly, 1968), pp. 157–66.
7. Gregory J. Rathjen, "The Impact of Legal Education on the Beliefs, Attitudes, and Values of Law Students," *Tennessee Law Review* 44 (1976): 95–101.
8. Scheingold, chaps. 1, 9, 10, 11.
9. Savoy, 460.
10. The coefficients reported in the table are squared multiple–partial correlation coefficients that eliminate the impact of regression to the mean (and thus overcome one of the main difficulties associated with the use of change data) by statistically controlling for the effect of Time 1 values of the dependent and independent variables. Editor's note: The data necessary to calculate the statistical significance of the coefficients in this table are not accessible.
11. The data reported in table 5.6 do not allow a comparison of the relative importance of the various independent variables included in the regression equations, but an examination of the unreported standardized regression coefficients revealed no clear pattern.
12. Since the effects of these changes in political identification and professional attitudes appear to be much less important than the changes in values and expectations focused on in the previous chapters, I do not pursue the question of what *caused* the changes identified here.
13. Howard S. Erlanger and Douglas A. Klegon, "Socialization Effects of Professional School: The Law School Experience and Student Orientations to Public Interest Concerns," *Law and Society Review* 13 (Fall, 1978): 32.
14. The proper measure of variance explained is the square of the partial

multiple correlation coefficient. Since the data to make that calculation are not accessible, the variance explained was estimated by taking the square of the standardized regression coefficient.

15. The reader might wonder whether controlling for additional independent variables would reduce the strength of the relationship between perceived employability and job preference. I did run regressions controlling for the values and expectations discussed in the previous chapters and found that the coefficients were significantly reduced. However, this reduction is consistent with the hypothesis that the reduction in employment confidence was *through* the effect that student employment and course work had on values and expectations.

    Another explanation, based on changing perceptions of the market, might argue that during law school the students simply learned that the salary gap between public interest and traditional jobs is larger than they had imagined, and they then adjusted their desires accordingly. However, I do not believe this to be a significant factor. Previously reported analysis based on these data conceptualized and operationalized job preferences in the economists' sense of that term—as underlying utility functions, which depict the degree of attraction for a particular job in terms of all job attributes except relative salary. The results of my analysis showed that the number of students who would be likely to accept public interest job offers at various specific, inflation-controlled salary levels declined substantially between Time 1 and Time 2. The shifts were similar in magnitude to those shown by the less sophisticated measures reported in chapter 2 and employed throughout this book. Robert V. Stover, "The Importance of Economic Supply in Determining the Size and Quality of the Public Interest Bar," *Law and Society Review* 16 (1981–82): 465–77

6 Preservers of the Hearth
Subcultural Support and the Role of the Law School

The Importance of Subcultural Support of Public Interest Work

Louie Littell flipped shut the casebook he'd been reading and headed for the library door. It was almost noon—time to eat and time for a meeting. Ascending the stairs from the second to the third floor of the law school, Louie observed the notice that he had hurriedly scrawled in red marking pen and posted at the landing earlier that morning: Lawyers Guild Meeting, Noon Today, Room 208. At the top of the stairs, he entered the "Sky Lounge," so named by an earlier generation of students for its unmistaken resemblance to countless airport coffee shops. Minutes later, sandwich and soft drink in hand, Louie scanned the snack bar for Guild types, found one whom he quickly reminded about the meeting, and then descended the stairs.

The meeting was in progress when I joined it fifteen minutes later. Five or six students, most in longish hair and blue jeans, occupied Room 208's forty seats. Presiding at the front stood Louie, slender and dark, balanced slightly more on one foot than the other, gesturing with his hand, and smiling beneath his thin dark mustache and wire-rimmed glasses. He might have been laying plans to protest racial discrimination in Colorado's bar examination; he might have been organizing a delegation to a regional conference of the Guild, or reporting on the local chapter's police repression project. In any case, he was doing what he did best—organizing and activating like-minded people.

Louie had begun law school a year and a half earlier with nagging doubts as to whether he was heading in a direction that was right for him. After graduating from a top southern university, he earned a master's degree in American poetry at an English university, trained as a chef, and worked organizing activities in the arts at a state penal farm under a grant from the federal government. In responding to my first questionnaire, he characterized himself as a political radical although his previous political experience did not extend beyond precinct work for George McGovern in the 1972 election. He began law school hoping to maintain his involvement in the arts through public interest legal activity of one sort or another, but he was uncertain whether this would be possible. As an alternative, he was interested in the practice of poverty law.

At the end of his law school career, Louie's commitment to public interest practice was firm. The job on my list of twenty which he designated as most preferable was "Attorney for an organization working to protect the rights of a racial minority group, such as the Native American Rights Fund or the NAACP." The two real-world employers he seriously considered were a small, left-oriented law firm with a heavy commitment to public interest law, and the Bay Area Lawyers for the Arts, an organization committed to providing legal services for the San Francisco Bay area's large community of struggling artists.

Central to Louie's continued commitment to public interest law were the support and encouragement he received through his involvement with the National Lawyers Guild. Louie attended meetings of the student chapter of the Guild from early in his first year of law school. As the year progressed, he joined other Guild members in demonstrating at the Denver City Council to protest police misconduct, leafleting at the law school in support of a strong affirmative action program, and representing initially unsuccessful applicants at hearings for unemployment compensation. By his second year in law school, Louie was the driving force in the student chapter and active in the more broadly based Denver chapter. Through his activity, Louie made and solidified friendships with a small core of similarly minded law students and lawyers. This circle of friends and acquaintances was crucial in insulating Louie from the sorts of changes in values and expectations that accompanied the decline in public interest concern among some of his classmates.

Refuge in the Lawyers Guild or some other public interest subculture appears to have been an important factor in differentiating those students who retained an initial preference for public interest practice from those who did not. In chapter 2, I reported that the number of students preferring public interest practice over other types of work was reduced by half during the law school years. The subsequent chapters posed the question, How can we account for the behavior of those students who turned away from a preference for public interest practice? and answered it by focusing on the process through which contact with the dominant professional culture eroded support for public interest practice. The present chapter asks, How can we explain the behavior of those students who *retained* their original public interest preference? and focuses on the countervailing effect of contact with a public interest subculture. I conclude that significant exposure to a public interest subculture was closely associated with the retention of an initial preference for public interest practice among DU students.

Of course, direct contact with a public interest subculture is not the only way in which students can be insulated from the eroding influence of the dominant professional culture; another is identification with a physically remote reference group.[1] Allison Smith, for example, relied on a small group of friends in another state and on her own robust self-concept to buttress her initial commitment to public interest practice. No doubt, there are other factors as well. Nonetheless, this chapter will focus on the relationship between significant contact with a public interest subculture and retention of an initial desire to practice public interest law. One reason I focus on the public interest subculture is that it is capable of being changed by reformers.

Three "Public Interest Centers." Chapters 3 and 4 described how contact with the dominant professional culture contributed to important changes in students' values and expectations. Two elements of that process of socialization stand in particularly sharp contrast to the process of socialization in the public interest subcultures I observed. First, the dominant professional culture—as manifest in both the law school and the broader legal community—did not communicate a sense of meaningful commitment to the norm of professional altruism. While the norm was not openly disparaged, direct expressions of support for the professional obligation to serve the disadvantaged were, with few exceptions, limited to ritualistic invocations at ceremonial occasions. Second, the dominant legal community appears to have conveyed to students an image of public interest ineptitude and marginality—the conventional mythology of public interest practice. In contrast, the centers of public interest support described in this chapter were supportive of public interest values and of a more positive image of public interest practice. Contact with these public interest subcultures provided students with valuable role models and with a sense of membership in a broader public interest community.

At the time of my study, I observed three primary points of institutionalized contact between DU students and public interest subcultures. At the law school itself, two relatively small overlapping groups of students provided support for public interest values and expectations. These were the Student Law Office and the student chapter of the National Lawyers Guild. Beyond the confines of the law school, the main source of support for the students' public interest aspirations came through work for a public interest organization such as a public defender or legal services office. Some students held paying positions with these organizations, while others received academic credit through the law school's internship and externship programs.

The Student Law Office stood at the center of the DU program in clinical legal education. Under Colorado's student practice rule, law students may, with the approval of the court, represent criminal defendants in misdemeanor and city ordinance cases. In a cooperative arrangement with the law school, Denver area courts channel large numbers of indigent defendants in such cases to the Student Law Office. There, acting under the supervision of a faculty member, second- and third-year law students perform all of the functions of a full-fledged attorney, including investigation, plea negotiation, and trial of cases. During the period of my study, student attorneys could receive academic credit for this work. In addition, experienced student attorneys could obtain paid positions as coordinators, helping to supervise beginning student attorneys and administering the flow of cases through the office.

Nineteen of the 103 students in my panel spent at least one academic quarter at the Student Law Office. Nine of these continued with the program beyond that point for periods ranging up to a total of six quarters for one individual. The law school promoted the Student Law Office primarily as an opportunity to gain litigation experience, not as an opportunity to do public service work. During the single quarter I participated in the program, the supervising faculty strongly emphasized the professional obligation of competent and vigorous representation, but not specifically in the context of *pro bono* service. Furthermore, of the nineteen members of my panel who participated in the program, nine did not express a preference for public interest practice either at the beginning or the end of law school.[2] Nevertheless, the proportion of students in the program who *were* enthusiastic about public interest law provided a critical mass large enough to draw the expression of support for professional altruism into the universe of ordinary student discourse.

Similarly, the dominant tone of discussion conveyed a distinctly positive image of public interest practice. When informally discussing public interest practice, many students and some faculty members spoke with an enthusiasm and pride that communicated a clear sense of challenge and potential accomplishment. Through words, tone of voice, facial expression, and body language, public interest practice was portrayed as providing ample opportunities for craft satisfaction, a reasonably effective means of helping the disadvantaged and working for social reform, and a source of experience, knowledge, and contacts beneficial to one's career.

In addition, the Student Law Office appeared to provide an important sense of community for students alienated by the dominant professional culture. As noted in chapter 3, students with a public interest orientation sometimes perceived themselves as isolated from the broader law school community. Those who found their way to the Student Law Office appeared to gain a sense of membership in a kindred community and, as a result, to regain a sense of confidence in their initial commitment to public interest law.

The second center of public interest support within the law school community was the student chapter of the National Lawyers Guild which was closely associated with the Denver chapter, a group that included many practicing attorneys with some history of public interest practice. The members of the student and Denver chapters worked together on a variety of projects and frequently socialized with each other at jointly sponsored social events. Many student members of the Guild also participated in the Student Law Office, but most of the students associated with the Law Office were not involved in the Guild. Only 5 of the 103 students in my panel were closely enough associated with the Guild to mention participation in the group's activities in response to two open-ended questions inquiring about undertakings of that nature during their law school years. Association with the Guild potentially shaped the perspective of student members in at least two interrelated ways: members freely communicated support for public interest values and expectations to one another, thus reinforcing their common views and sense of shared identity and commitment, and the Guild provided role models of attorneys actively involved in public interest practice.

The experience of Louie Littell, mentioned at the start of the chapter, illustrates the degree to which membership in an organization like the Guild can solidify a student's commitment to public interest law. Louie entered law school with a rather diffuse commitment to both left-wing politics and public interest practice. His own explanation of his developing commitment to public interest practice emphasized the crystallization of his political beliefs. In the winter of his first year of law school, he joined a study group led by a third-year student with strong Guild ties. In addition to the Guild activities summarized at the beginning of the chapter, Louie attended three national meetings of the Guild at which he participated in extensive debate and discussion of both domestic and international political issues. By the end of his final year of law school Louie's earlier diffuse and noncommittal political orientation had sharpened and solidified into a well-defined point of view. Many of his answers to my questions were couched in terms that he sometimes referred to as "Guild analysis." For example, his written response to a question about changes in his political attitudes during law school stated,

> I suspect the most dramatic change in these areas is the question of civil liberties and the politics underlying these that have been revealed to me through legal study and Guild activism. There is a striking demarcation in the rights that will and will not be protected by our state apparatus. Enforcement of civil liberties is selective and class-oriented. . . . [This] revelation has changed my views on the pursuit of limited civil liberties ends.

Although there is no necessary connection between ideology and behavior, Louie's political beliefs clearly strengthened his desire for public interest practice. Unwilling to work for a conventional law firm and not content to rely on channels such as the law school's placement office to locate a politically acceptable alternative, Louie sought out and cultivated the Bay Area Lawyers for the Arts as a potential employer.

Louie's membership in the Guild also solidified his commitment to public interest law in other ways. The support and encouragement he received from other members was mentioned earlier in the chapter. In addition, Louie's attendance at the national meetings was particularly important in establishing the Guild as a positive reference group and in providing Louie with viable role models. Even in a community as large as Denver, the number of Guild attorneys actively involved in the type of highly politicized public interest practice that Louie found appealing probably did not exceed half a dozen. Through the Guild, Louie attached himself to a nationwide network of such attorneys. Louie described the importance of his first such exposure (during the summer after his first year of law school) as follows:

> The Guild convention this summer was invaluable in that I met dozens but saw a thousand or so attorneys who were all . . . radical lawyers—who . . . all seem politically dynamic and see themselves making a legitimate contribution towards what they believe in. If it *has* been done, it makes it a lot easier for someone who might harbor similar convictions—in hoping that I can do the same type of thing, that I'll be able to get by—that I'm not alone. I'm not fighting by myself at all.

Most of the students involved with the Lawyers Guild were neither as active as Louie nor as deeply affected by the experience. Louie, however, was not unique. During my three years in law school, I observed students in cohorts ahead of and behind mine who were affected in much the same way.

The third point of contact with public interest subcultures was through law-related work with a public interest organization. Some students were paid for this work, and others received academic credit through the law school's internship and externship programs, for which DU was quite liberal in granting credit. My questionnaire identified twenty-two students who did work of this type. Nine of the twenty-two worked for either a public defender office or a legal services office. The others worked with a wide variety of organizations including, for example, the American Civil Liberties Union, Women in Crisis, the conservative Mountain States Legal Foundation, the Native American Center of the Cheyenne and Arapaho Tribe, and the Thursday Night Bar (private attorneys who donated Thursday evenings to *pro bono* legal service for the poor). All of these jobs included at least some contact with practicing attorneys and, thus, the opportunity to see and hear support for professional altruism and to form a favorable image of public interest employment.

In sum, contact with a public interest subculture appears to have insulated students from the influence of the dominant culture in several ways. First, the alternative professional communities communicated support for the norm of professional altruism. Second, they conveyed an image of public interest practice sharply at odds with the prevailing image of public interest ineptitude and marginality. Third, they provided altruistically oriented students with the assurance that they were not alone in their beliefs but belonged to a broader community of like-minded persons. Fourth, they provided students with role models. And fifth, in the case of the Lawyers Guild, contact with a public interest subculture provided some students with a political point of view that heightened their commitment to public interest goals.

Quantitative Analysis of the Influence of Public Interest Subcultures. If my analysis is correct, then those students with significant exposure to a public interest subculture should have been more likely than others to retain any initial preference for public interest practice. Table 6.1, while based on limited data, allows us to explore this hypothesis by examining the experiences of the thirty-eight students who at the beginning of law school indicated some interest in public interest practice.[3] The table shows the relationship between exposure to one of the public interest "centers" discussed earlier (Student Law Office, National Lawyers Guild, and part-time work with a public interest employer) and retention of a preference for a public interest job at graduation. While the numbers are small, the results are striking. All 6 of those students exposed to two or three of the centers of public interest subculture retained their initial preference for public interest law, as did 6 out of 14 (43%) exposed to one of the centers. In contrast, only 5 out of 18 (28%) exposed to none of the centers retained their public interest preference. The strength of this relationship, as measured by Kendall's Tau, was strong and statistically significant.

While the data are consistent with the argument that significant exposure to a public interest subculture plays an important role in insulating students from the eroding influence of the dominant professional culture, my analysis is limited by the fact that I cannot establish the causal order of the relationship. For example, students who by the end of the first year had entirely lost their initial desire for public interest practice probably were less likely than those who had retained that desire to initiate contact with public interest groups; thus, it may be that strong preference for public interest employment leads to affiliation with the public interest "centers" rather than vice versa. To

Table 6.1 Public Interest Subcultures and Preference for Public Interest Practice

Preference for Public Interest Practice at Graduation	Number of Public Interest Centers with which Student Had Contact			
	None	One	Two	Three
No	72% (13)	57% (8)	0	0
Yes	28% (5)	43% (6)	100% (5)	100% (1)
	100% (18)	100% (14)	100% (5)	100% (1)

Note: Data for thirty-eight students who expressed preference for public interest work at the start of law school; Kendall's Tau C = .45; $p < .05$.

fully unravel the relationship would require data on the students' job preferences at the beginning of the second and third years. In the absence of that information, we must rely primarily on the more impressionistic observations, which support the hypothesis that subcultural exposure affects job preferences rather than vice versa.

Factors Limiting Contact with Public Interest Subcultures. It is important to emphasize that most students were not affected by exposure to a public interest subculture, because only 36 of the 103 students in my panel had contact with any of the three centers. For 7 of those 36 students, that exposure was limited to a single ten-week academic quarter at the Student Law Office. And for at least 8 others, it was limited to three months or less of work with some other public interest organization.[4] Only 9 students were exposed to more than one center.

The figures are perhaps more striking if attention is focused on the 38 students who at the beginning of their law school careers expressed some preference for public interest practice. Eighteen students—or 47% of this group of students most likely to desire exposure to a public interest subculture—failed to intersect with *any* of the three institutionalized points of contact. And the exposure of at least 7 others was limited either to a single quarter at the Student Law Office or to three months or less of work with some other public interest organization.[5] Only 6 of the 38 made contact with two or three centers of public interest support.

As I noted in the last section, this lack of exposure might be attributable to the students' own preferences. Wouldn't those who truly desired contact with a public interest subculture somehow have found their way to the Student Law Office, the Lawyers Guild, or part-time employment with a public interest organization? Perhaps. But this explanation would ignore the subcultural and behavioral constraints that discouraged some students from associating with the public interest centers.

The opportunities for first-year students to make contact with centers of public interest support were especially limited. The rules of the Law School prohibited their participation in the Student Law Office. And lacking the knowledge and skills of second- and third-year students, they were not likely to find law-related work with a public interest organization outside the law school. But perhaps even more importantly, few first-year students would have wanted these involvements. As emphasized in chapter 3, most beginning law students direct so much time and energy to meeting the stress of the first year that they withdraw from other activities. The Lawyers Guild did its best to attract first-year students, but was relatively unsuccessful, in part because it did not address itself to their needs. Any public interest organization that does not somehow provide help in coping with the demanding first-year environment is almost certain to be ignored by beginning law students. On the other hand, a public interest organization that somehow succeeded in attracting large numbers of first-year students might do much to cushion the impact of the first year on altruistic values.

The constraints on contact by second- and third-year students varied. First, consider the Student Law Office, where the extremely demanding nature of the program appeared to discourage some students from participating at all, while motivating others to limit the duration of their participation. In my single academic quarter at the office, I devoted twenty to thirty hours a week to the program for four hours of academic credit. Although the cases were minor, and most were ultimately disposed of by a plea bargain, generally the supervising faculty pushed the students to treat each case as a complete learning experience. The faculty member who supervised my work required students to file numerous motions, such as for suppression of evidence, and to research and write legal briefs in support of each motion. Although only one of my four cases went to trial, I prepared fully for trial for two others not disposed of until the trial date.

Students wishing to continue with the program for more than two academic quarters could not receive academic credit but could obtain paid positions as student coordinators. The time demanded of coordinators in supervising beginning students and other tasks varied greatly depending on the faculty member and the student attorneys with whom they worked. In all cases the effective hourly wage the coordinators received was substantially less than they would have made in a conventional clerking job. Of the 103 students in my panel, 10 participated in the program for one quarter, 4 for two quarters, and 5 for three or more. In sum, students who needed well-paid part-time jobs—or who for other reasons were unable or unwilling to meet the substantial time demands of the Student Law Office—were unlikely to participate in the program for more than one quarter, if at all.

The factors discouraging student involvement with the Lawyers Guild were of an entirely different nature. Members could devote as much or as little time to Guild activities as they desired. Meetings, held during the noon hour at the law school, were open to anyone who chose to attend, as was participation in Guild projects, protests, and parties. But the Guild's political stance placed strong constraints on its ability to serve large numbers of students as an effective point of contact with a public interest subculture. As noted in chapter 3, an orientation meeting for the student chapter early in my first year attracted seven students whom I recognized as classmates, and probably as many more first-year students whom I failed to recognize. By the middle of the first quarter, no more than one or two first-year students attended meetings. This decrease can be attributed in part to the pressure of the hectic first year. But the fact that most of those students showing an early interest in Guild activity failed to return even during the more relaxed second and third years of law school must be attributed in part to the organization's image of strident radicalism and to its concern with a broad range of international political issues that many students considered irrelevant to the practice of public interest law. In addition, the reputation of the student chapter was hurt by the fact that a few years earlier the Denver Guild had taken political stands that alienated feminist and gay-rights advocates.

All nine of the students I interviewed in depth for this study had at some point in their law school careers at least a tentative interest in the Guild, but only three participated meaningfully in Guild activities. The others were discouraged from associating by various elements of the organization's political stance. Barbara Phillips told me that she was "not really excited at the consciousness of the Guild as it pertains to women" and that she had "other things to do than work with that." Allison Smith was concerned that "their emphasis was starting to be very international and into politics in South America and things like that." Nelson Fixx complained about what he perceived as hypocritical radicalism, referring in particular to a student who was

> born to money, father a rich executive, yet a member of the Lawyers Guild . . . and seems to be very down on the things that put her where she is financially. Well, those attitudes seem to me not formed out of living through the conflicts that they're now trying to battle with words, but they're rather a bit phony—hypocritical—and that turns me off.

A number of classmates, including Ellen Torgeson, indicated displeasure with the "rhetoric" of the Guild and the tendency of members to use radical clichés in a sweeping analysis of society's ills.

In short, the highly politicized approach that attracted Louie Littell and solidified his preference for public interest law appeared to repel many potential public interest lawyers. As important as it was for some students, the Guild was not able to serve as an effective support group for most of those who started law school with a preference for public interest practice.

The third opportunity, working with a public interest organization outside the law school, appeared to be subject to fewer constraints than either of the other two opportunities for contact I have discussed. First of all, the time commitment was often much less than that of the Student Law Office. In addition, the variety of positions available ensured that most students could find an ideologically compatible organization. The limited number of paid positions with public interest organizations appeared to restrict the number of students able to supplement their income through such activity, but the law school's willingness to grant academic credit for such work provided an alternative for many students. Perhaps as a result of these factors, 14 of the 38 students initially preferring public interest practice were able to do law-related work for a public interest organization at some point during their law school career—compared to only 9 from this group who worked for the Student Law Office and 4 who affiliated with the Lawyers Guild.

Nonetheless, there were constraints on this activity. Although working for a public interest organization was usually less time-consuming than working at the Student Law Office, the hours were frequently substantial. Fifteen of the 19 students who provided the relevant data worked an average of at least fifteen hours a week at such jobs, and 10 worked an average of at least twenty hours a week.[6] As a result, students who failed to secure one of the small number of paid public interest positions—and thus needed to take a job with a conventional law firm— probably would have had difficulty finding the time needed for most public interest internships. These constraints may also help account for the fact that no more than 9 of 103 students worked with a public interest organization for a period exceeding three months. Finally, although the intern and extern programs played an important role in encouraging students to work for public interest organizations, the law school promoted the program in a rather low-key manner and did not actively recruit participants.

To summarize, the constraints on contact with a public interest subculture were especially great for first-year students, but also discouraged second- and third-year students. All three centers of public interest support were subject to behavioral or structural constraints that restricted the number of students making significant contact with them or limited the duration of that contact. No center of public interest support was both situated at the law school and only moderately demanding of students' time, while at the same time ideologically compatible with a broad range of political beliefs.

I do not mean to argue that DU should reduce the work required of students participating in the Student Law Office program or that the Lawyers Guild should alter its political stance. Both of those institutions serve important functions in their present form. But if law schools are to stem the tide away from public interest practice, they must provide additional institutional structures capable of reaching a broader range of public interest–oriented students early in their law school careers.

Between the Bookends: What the Law Schools Can Do

Now comes the hard part, I thought. I had just finished the draft of all but this last section. Satisfied that it was ready for the typist, I slipped the manuscript back into its folder and deposited it in my briefcase. Leaning back in my chair, I looked over at my thirteen-year-old daughter, sitting on the couch doing homework. I had begun work on this project when she was six, started law school when she was seven, graduated when she was nine, spent the next three-and-a-half years just trying to figure out what had happened and putting it in writing—and *now* comes the hard part!

Describing what's wrong with an institution is easy. Even explaining *why* isn't so bad, at least if you've got enough data to make it look like you know what you're talking about. But making suggestions for reform that will be taken seriously is an entirely different matter. People will not be responsive to proposals for change unless they are convinced that a problem exists and believe that the solutions I suggest can help to solve the problem.

The preceding chapters have shown that a problem exists, and have explained its source by focusing on changes in values and changes in expectations about the opportunities that different jobs provide to achieve those values. In this chapter, I have argued that *subcultural support* is the key element in this process. The values, images, and myths of the dominant professional culture receive a good deal of support within and outside the law school, while structural support for altruistic values and public interest practice—while present—is weak and scattered. Thus, in setting forth my proposals for change, I focus on the ways in which subcultural support for public interest work can be focused and strengthened.

The purpose of these proposals is not to remake the law school into a predominantly public interest–oriented institution, although I admire the efforts of the law schools at Antioch and Queens College of CUNY to do so.[7] I take it for granted that the typical curriculum will remain heavily weighted toward conventional, business-oriented legal practice. But at the same time, the reforms I suggest are not small ones. They will not be accomplished without substantial and sustained effort on the part of law school faculty and administrators or without a sincere commitment by the practicing bar to lend assistance.

Subcultural Support. Law schools committed to fostering support for public interest practice should attempt to increase the number of students exposed to a public interest subculture. The most efficient means to this end might be to establish and nurture a broadly based public interest student group. The primary goal of this group would be to provide support for students who enter law school hoping to practice public interest law, and not necessarily to convert students whose job preferences run in other directions. The organization should attempt to insulate its members from the effects of the dominant professional culture by encouraging them to feel part of a community of public interest concern, by providing them with public interest role models, and by exposing them to a broad range of support for public interest values and expectations.

The organization should be structured for maximum appeal to its natural constituency. A concerted effort should be made to emphasize accessibility by minimizing structural and behavioral constraints to participation. The organization should eschew ideological narrowness. Groups with a distinct political focus, such as the National Lawyers Guild, play an important role, but they attract a small following. The organization I envision would direct its appeal to as broad a spectrum of altruistically oriented students as possible; its primary emphasis would be on public interest law, not on political ideology.

Even more importantly, the organization should foster accessibility by making its activities convenient and useful to students. Law students face a multiplicity of competing demands. A broadly based public interest organization must accommodate students' busy schedules by centering its activities at the law school and scheduling them at convenient times. The influence of the dominant culture is great because students are automatically immersed in it as they proceed through their normal daily routine of attending classes. The influence of a public interest subculture, on the other hand, will be felt primarily by students who act affirmatively to make contact with it. A public interest student group must motivate students to join its activities by meeting their self-identified needs. And it surely will fail to attract its potential constituency if it appeals exclusively to their public interest concerns; too many forces pull students in other directions. First-year

students, for example, withdraw their attention from almost everything but coping with the stress of law school and generally shun activities that are not related to this need.

To be successful, a public interest organization must build support for public interest values and expectations through activities that respond to the academic, social, and psychological needs of law students. Among other projects, this organization should help students form study groups, sponsor social events which include members of the public interest bar, organize presentations on professional issues of particular importance to public interest practice, and coordinate information about public interest positions. On the surface, projects like helping students form study groups might seem unrelated to public interest concerns, but they are not. Study groups would bring public interest oriented students into contact with each other, which is important because study group members provide each other with important psychological support. The knowledge that others in the group share public interest concerns will relieve study group members of the feeling of isolation.

Influence within the Dominant Culture. Law schools should not limit their efforts at reform to nurturing public interest subcultures. In addition they should encourage a more active and open expression of support for public interest values and expectations within the dominant law school culture.

Perhaps most importantly, the law schools should lead by example, demonstrating to their students and to the private bar a commitment to serving the underrepresented. Faculty members might be required to devote time to *pro bono* representation, in a manner similar to proposals currently being considered for the practicing bar. A requirement for public interest practice might also be imposed on law students, perhaps beginning in the first year. Law students trained to deal with the legal issues affecting the underrepresented will find it much easier as lawyers to fulfill their public interest obligation. Students could work with public interest organizations,[8] private attorneys, professors, or more advanced students in projects such as the Student Law Office at DU.

In addition, the law schools could place students in a variety of positions that would less directly involve service on behalf of the underrepresented but still would emphasize public service in a professional capacity. Examples would include bailiff work for judges; legal clerkships with prosecutors' offices; research service for state legislators, city council members, state and local government agencies, and

perhaps even college student governments; and working for corrections agencies, such as probation and parole departments, or for pretrial release agencies.

Although not without potential problems, a more innovative approach would follow the lead of a program at the Case Western Reserve Medical School, where at the beginning of the first year, each medical student was assigned to follow a mother during the last trimester of her pregnancy, stay with her throughout her labor and delivery, and then serve primarily as a pediatrician (in training) for the baby.[9] Law students could be assigned to indigent families, at first to bring their legal needs to the attention of practicing attorneys, and then in the second and third year of law school, to participate in legal services such as preparing tax returns, drafting wills, dealing with creditors and welfare agencies, and so forth.

Finally, a law school could produce additional opportunities for students to fulfill their public interest obligation (and at the same time further demonstrate its own commitment) by creating one or more new public interest agencies under its own aegis. For example, with the financial help of the private bar, a law school might establish a poverty law research center, which might act as a back-up center for local attorneys.[10]

Providing the hundreds of students at most law schools with the opportunity to do public interest work will not be easy. At a minimum, it would take several years to develop the network of contacts needed to make such a program fully operational, but the idea should not be rejected as impractical until a genuine effort has been made. Over time, as such efforts in the law school succeed in producing law graduates willing to fulfill their public interest obligation as lawyers, it will become increasingly easy to pair students with attorneys in public interest activities.

There are also a number of small ways in which a law school could demonstrate a commitment to professional altruism to its students. Perhaps most importantly, the obligation to public interest service should be given a prominent place in the standard course on professional ethics. Scholarships—funded in whole or in part by the private bar—could be established for students committed to pursuing low-paying public interest jobs such as legal aid work. An institutional commitment to public interest values could be emphasized in law school catalogs and bulletins; applicants for admission to law school and for financial assistance could be required to affirm their willingness to meet the professional obligation of *pro bono* service. In these and a myriad of other ways, a law school could begin to bring the commu-

nication of support for public interest practice into the universe of conventional discourse in the dominant culture.

The discussion so far has emphasized programs and policies that could be implemented by law school administrators, sometimes with the assistance of the private bar. There are also ways in which sympathetic faculty members could modify their teaching approach so as to convey a greater degree of support for public interest values and expectations. I am not asking faculty members to advance beliefs that they do not themselves accept. I am simply asking those faculty members whose values and expectations are supportive of public interest practice to teach in a way what communicates this to their students.

As emphasized in chapter 3, the typical law student is exposed to an environment which largely ignores altruistic values while emphasizing a broad range of other concerns. And in chapter 4, I showed how students are bombarded with a variety of cues that suggest images of ineptitude and marginality for public interest practice and images of excellence for large corporate practice. Many DU faculty members privately rejected these values and expectations, but in the classroom, these professors generally reinforced them by their silence. Infatuated by Langdellian scientism, they neglected the professional obligation to serve the disadvantaged. But if supporters of public interest practice do not try to counterbalance the messages of the dominant culture, nobody will. Quick but clear statements of the importance of public interest practice can be inserted in discussions of cases involving impecunious parties or potential awards not large enough to justify normal attorney's fees.

Of course, this strategy will not work unless a professor employs cases, hypotheticals, or personal examples concerning impecunious clients, less than princely damages, or reform- or cause-oriented litigation on behalf of the otherwise unrepresented. Professors should not hesitate to draw on their own experience (or that of others) on behalf of the underrepresented when illustrating legal concepts. This practice will not only demonstrate their commitment to public interest values; it will also help to combat the myth of public interest ineptitude and marginality. In addition, using public interest hypotheticals and examples creates a moment in which professors can unobtrusively mention the opportunities for *pro bono* practice provided by various bar association programs and by groups like the American Civil Liberties Union.

Finally, professors who are committed to the importance of a strong public interest bar should take care not to inadvertently discourage students from public interest careers by subtly echoing the dominant professional culture's fascination with the pecuniary rewards of legal practice and with service on behalf of the rich and the powerful.

A Brief Word on the Demand for Public Interest Attorneys. If the reforms I have suggested are effective in increasing the size and quality of the full-time public interest bar (as opposed to simply increasing *pro bono* practice by private attorneys), they will increase the supply of potential public interest lawyers.[11] But in addition, law schools might attempt to stimulate demand for public interest lawyers by joining with bar associations to sponsor and fund public interest law firms, by goading large private firms to hire attorneys whose efforts would be devoted entirely to public interest practice, or by similar efforts to raise the consciousness and commitment of the private bar to the profession's public interest obligation.

Conclusion

The major premise of this book is that lawyers and law schools have a professional obligation to ensure adequate legal representation for individuals and interests who would lack that representation if they had to rely exclusively on their own resources. Without adequate legal representation, parties with valid claims may never know or assert their rights and, even if they do, may find themselves overwhelmed by the superior resources of the rich and the powerful. The ABA's recently adopted *Model Rules of Professional Conduct* states that "A lawyer should render public interest service."[12] I would add that every law school, regardless of competing budgetary demands or grumbling students and faculty, should act to at least maintain whatever commitment to public interest practice its students have when they enter.

Meeting this challenge will not be easy. The fact that the law schools' responsibility to act does not spring from their own misfeasance only serves to make the task more arduous. The drift away from public interest practice among law students is the product of many factors, some of which law schools are unable to control. If they are to succeed in slowing or arresting this drift, law schools must not only eliminate the effects of those factors which they can control, but they must also offset or counterbalance the effects of those variables which they cannot control.

Law faculties and administrators possess the experience, intellectual acumen, and creative energy to produce and implement programs for reform superior to those I have proposed. My only fear is that even those faculties most sympathetic to the need for change will succumb to the temptation to limit reform to measures most easily accomplished, and will ignore the measures that require the greatest commitment of resources or meet the greatest resistance on grounds of personal inconvenience. Little good can come of such timidity.

Not every idea for change will product the expected results. Success, if it comes at all, will not come quickly but only after a good deal of creative experimentation. But the rewards will be great, at least for those who believe in the ideal of true equality before the law. These rewards will spring from nothing less than a full-fledged effort at reform. The time to begin that effort is now.

NOTES

1. For example, Theodore M. Newcomb, "Attitude Development as a Function of Reference Groups: The Bennington Study," in Guy E. Swanson, Theodore M. Newcomb, and Eugene Hartley, eds., *Readings in Social Psychology* (New York: Holt, 1952), pp. 420–30; Robert K. Merton, "Continuities in the Theory of Reference Groups and Social Structure," in his book *Social Theory and Social Structure*, enlarged edition (New York: Free Press, 1968), pp. 335–440.
2. This figure reflects the number of students who did not even ambiguously express a preference for public interest practice at either the beginning or end of law school in answering the open-ended question about employment preferences.
3. Preference for public interest practice was in response to the open-ended question about employment preferences. Limiting the analysis to the thirty-eight students who expressed some indication of preference for a public interest job at the beginning of law school makes sense for two reasons. First, as reported in chapter 2, only two students who did *not* express a preference for public interest practice at Time 1 changed to do so at Time 2. Second, holding Time 1 preferences constant avoids the potentially distorting effects of statistical regression to the mean.

   An analysis parallel to that reported in table 6.1, but which coded the job preference variable so as to require a more definite expression of preference for public interest practice, produced results essentially the same as those reported here.
4. Three more students pursued public interest internships of undetermined duration.
5. Two more students in this group pursued public interest internships of undetermined duration.
6. These figures include three students who worked forty to sixty hours a week on externships for which they received sixteen hours of academic credit.

7. See John M., Farago, "The Pedagogy of Community: Trust and Responsibility at CUNY Law School," *Nova Law Journal* 10 (1986): 465–94 and Charles R. Halpern, "A New Direction in Legal Education: The CUNY Law School at Queens College," *Nova Law Journal* 10 (1986): 549–74. See also, generally, Daniel Pollitt, "A Law School with a Bent for Public Service," *Nova Law Journal* 10 (1986): 779–92.
8. It would be unfortunate if the result of an increase in uncompensated *pro bono* work by students were a reduction in the number of paid clerking jobs offered to students by public interest employers. Replacing paid law clerks, most of whom sought out those jobs because they possessed some initial preference for public interest practice, with unpaid students drawn more or less randomly from the broader student population would eliminate an important source of subcultural support for those law clerks and perhaps force them into the clerking market for conventional law firms, thus increasing the probability that they would drift away from public interest law. Therefore it would be important for the law school to attempt to reach an understanding with such employers concerning the continuation of paid positions.
9. Benjamin Spock, "Coercion in the Classroom Won't Work," *The Atlantic* 253 (April, 1984): 29.
10. In some respects these offices might play a role similar to that performed by the Legal Services Corporation's national and state support centers, but there is little danger of superfluity in light of the extreme budgetary constraints faced by Legal Services.
11. Robert V. Stover, "The Importance of Economic Supply in Determining the Size and Quality of the Public Interest Bar," *Law and Society Review* 16 (1981–82): 458–65.
12. American Bar Association, *Model Rules of Professional Conduct* (adopted 1983), Rule 6.1.

Appendix
Questionnaire

Job Choice by New Attorneys Questionnaire Survey

A Study of Denver University Law Students
Conducted by Dr. Robert V. Stover, September 1977

-1-

For Questions 1 through 9, circle the answer that best represents your views.

1. More should be done to protect the position of the consumer relative to that of businesses that produce and distribute goods and services.

   1. Strongly agree 2. Agree 3. Undecided 4. Disagree 5. Strongly disagree

2. More should be done to protect the environment against abuses by big business and others.

   1. Strongly agree 2. Agree 3. Undecided 4. Disagree 5. Strongly disagree

3. More should be done to protect the interests of business against the challenge posed by activists claiming to represent environmental and consumer concerns.

   1. Strongly agree 2. Agree 3. Undecided 4. Disagree 5. Strongly disagree

4. More should be done to protect the economic and social position of the middle class.

   1. Strongly agree 2. Agree 3. Undecided 4. Disagree 5. Strongly disagree

5. More should be done to improve the economic and social position of Blacks, Chicanos, Native Americans, and other racial minorities.

   1. Strongly agree 2. Agree 3. Undecided 4. Disagree 5. Strongly disagree

6. More should be done to provide for the needs of persons living below or close to the poverty level.

   1. Strongly agree 2. Agree 3. Undecided 4. Disagree 5. Strongly disagree

7. It is important that big business continue to play a major role in the American system.

   1. Strongly agree 2. Agree 3. Undecided 4. Disagree 5. Strongly disagree

8. More should be done to protect basic civil liberties such as freedom of speech, press, and religion, and the rights of persons espousing unpopular views.

   1. Strongly agree 2. Agree 3. Undecided 4. Disagree 5. Strongly disagree

9. More should be done to protect the economic and property rights of business against governmental regulation and control.

   1. Strongly agree 2. Agree 3. Undecided 4. Disagree 5. Strongly disagree

-2-

10. Listed below are 21 job attributes that you may or may not desire to find in your initial full-time job after receiving your law degree. First, use Column 1 to rate on a ten-point scale the extent to which you desire to find each attribute in your initial job (10 = most highly desired; 1 = least highly desired). Then use Column 2 to rank order the five top-rated attributes, using a "1" to denote the first most desired attribute, a "2" to denote the second most desired, and so on to "5." Remember, in Column 1, high numbers denote greatest desirability, but in Column 2, low numbers do.

LIST OF ATTRIBUTES	Column 1 Rate desirability of attributes on 10-point scale. 10 = Most highly 1 = Least highly	Column 2 Rank desirability of attributes. 1 = 1st most 2 = 2nd most And so on to 5
Earn at least a moderate starting salary.......	______	______
Earn a high starting salary....................	______	______
Move to a high future salary...................	______	______
Have job security..............................	______	______
Live in the right geographical locale..........	______	______
Have time to satisfy off-the-job interests.....	______	______
Work for desired social and political goals....	______	______
Work in a congenial interpersonal atmosphere...	______	______
Control your own work and work schedule........	______	______
Work directly with clients.....................	______	______
Receive guidance from experienced attorneys....	______	______
Gain valuable experience, knowledge & contacts.	______	______
Advance professionally with initial employer...	______	______
Maintain flexibility for future job options....	______	______
Gain professional and/or community prestige....	______	______
Challenge your ability.........................	______	______
Work in areas of the law you find interesting..	______	______
Do innovative and creative work................	______	______
Especially use your professional legal skills..	______	______
Feel the satisfaction of producing results.....	______	______
Help persons or groups with whom you identify or sympathize................................	______	______

-3-

11. In a sentence or two, describe the form of employment which you would like most to have for your initial full-time job after receiving your law degree. (E.g., I hope to join a small firm specializing in business law and serving small and medium-sized businesses; or, I would like to be a public defender, serving criminal defendants in a metropolitan area.)

12. At this time, how would you rate your chances of finding this form of employment for your initial full-time job?

1.____Very good 2.____Fairly good 3.____Not very good

13. If your answer to Question 11 does not clearly state the area of law which you find most interesting, please describe it below.

14. On the next page are listed 20 different "job types" which may or may not include the job described by you in Question 11. Turn the page, read through the list, and circle the one that you would consider most preferable among those listed for your initial full-time job after graduating.

-4-

15. In Column 1, rate on a ten-point scale each job type listed below for its desirability as an initial job after graduating (10 = very desirable; 1 = very undesirable; LI = lack sufficient information to make an intelligent choice). Review the entire list before proceeding. After you have finished your ratings in Column 1, turn to page 6 to find instructions for Columns 2 and 3.

(1) Working for yourself as a solo practitioner, attempting to build a practice from whatever cases are available . . . .

(2) Attorney for a small law firm (2-6 attorneys) that specializes in business law . . . .

(3) Attorney for a small law firm (2-6 attorneys) with a general civil practice . . . .

(4) Attorney for a small law firm (2-6 attorneys) that specializes in criminal and personal injury litigation . . . .

(5) Attorney for a small law firm (2-6 attorneys) that does a large amount of free "public interest" law in addition to normal, income-producing work . .

(6) Attorney for a medium-sized law firm (10-16 attorneys) that specializes in business and corporate law . . . .

(7) Attorney for a medium-sized law firm (10-16 attorneys) with a general civil practice . . . .

(8) Attorney for a large law firm (20 or more attorneys) that specializes in corporate law . . . .

(9) House counsel for a large or medium-sized corporation . . . .

(10) Attorney for a non-profit "public interest" law center that specializes in environmental and consumer law . . . .

(11) Attorney for a "public interest lobby group" for which you did litigation, lobbying, investigative research, political organizing, and public relations .

(12) Staff attorney for the American Civil Liberties Union . . . .

(13) Attorney for an organization working to protect the rights of a racial minority group, such as the Native American Rights Fund or the NAACP . .

(14) Attorney for a typical state or local governmental agency . . . .

(15) Clerk for a state supreme court justice . . . .

(16) Deputy district attorney, prosecuting criminal cases . . . .

(17) Attorney for a public defender office, handling criminal cases for indigent defendants . . . .

(18) Attorney for a legal aid or legal services office, handling civil cases for poor persons . . . .

(19) Attorney for a federal agency in the social services area, such as Health, Education and Welfare or Housing and Urban Development . . . .

(20) Attorney for a federal regulatory agency, such as the Securities and Exchange Commission or the Interstate Commerce Commission . . . .

-5-

	Column 1	Column 2	Column 3
	Desirability of job on a 10-pt. scale. 10 = Very desirable 1 = Very *undesirable* LI = Lack suff. info.	Would you apply for job opening during job hunt? Y = Yes N = No LI = Lack suff. info.	Chances of getting offer. 3 = Very good 2 = Fairly good 1 = Not very good LI = Lack suff. info.
......	________	________	________
......	________	________	________
......	________	________	________
......	________	________	________
......	________	________	________
......	________	________	________
......	________	________	________
......	________	________	________
......	________	________	________
......	________	________	________
......	________	________	________
......	________	________	________
......	________	________	________
......	________	________	________
......	________	________	________
......	________	________	________
......	________	________	________
......	________	________	________
......	________	________	________
......	________	________	________

-6-

16. In Column 2 on page 5 indicate whether you would apply for each of the jobs listed if an opening were to occur during your search for an initial job after graduating (Y = yes; N = no; LI = lack sufficient information to make an intelligent choice).

17. In Column 3 on page 5 rate your chances of actually being offered each job if an opening were to occur and you were to apply for it (3 = very good; 2 = fairly good; 1 = not very good; LI = lack sufficient information to make an intelligent choice). Make this rating even if your answer in Column 2 states that in fact you would not apply for the job. In other words, for purposes of making this rating, assume you would apply.

18. Lawyers should be more concerned with solving technical legal problems than with solving broader political and social problems.

    1. Strongly agree 2. Agree 3. Undecided 4. Disagree 5. Strongly disagree

19. It is important that individual attorneys protect the public image of the legal profession by refraining from bizarre or unconventional behavior.

    1. Strongly agree 2. Agree 3. Undecided 4. Disagree 5. Strongly disagree

20. A lawyer should be willing to provide his services to all clients with a legitimate need for legal counsel, even if it means supporting political, economic, or social interests with which the lawyer disagrees.

    1. Strongly agree 2. Agree 3. Undecided 4. Disagree 5. Strongly disagree

21. In general, members of the legal profession deserve a high level of income.

    1. Strongly agree 2. Agree 3. Undecided 4. Disagree 5. Strongly disagree

22. A lawyer should be more concerned with protecting the interests of his individual clients than with trying to reform the law to improve society.

    1. Strongly agree 2. Agree 3. Undecided 4. Disagree 5. Strongly disagree

23. As an attorney, I would enjoy having a reputation among fellow members of the bar as being somewhat of a nonconformist.

    1. Strongly agree 2. Agree 3. Undecided 4. Disagree 5. Strongly disagree

24. The distinctive skills of the legal profession include ability in activities such as lobbying, investigative research, political organizing, and public relations.

    1. Strongly agree 2. Agree 3. Undecided 4. Disagree 5. Strongly disagree

-7-

25. All things considered, if forced to choose, I would classify my political ideology as:

    1._____Very conservative

    2._____Conservative

    3._____Moderate

    4._____Liberal

    5._____Very Liberal

    6._____Radical

26. Please describe any political activity in which you have engaged during the past five years beyond simply voting. Include both electoral and nonelectoral politics.

27. Beyond your answer to the previous question, is there any way in which during the past five years you have worked actively to achieve what you perceive (or did perceive) as a socially desirable goal--either for society as a whole or for some community or group extending beyond your immediate family? If so, please describe both your activity and the goal for which you were working.

28. Down the left-hand side of this page are listed eight of the 20 job types that you rated in terms of desirability for your inital full-time job after law school. Across the top of pages 8 through 11 are listed the 21 job attributes that you rated and ranked according to your desire to find them in your initial job. In answering the present question, you are to state a prediction concerning the likelihood that each attribute really would be found in each job. Do this by filling in the blanks on pages (continued at top of page 9)

	Work in areas of the law you find interesting	Maintain flexibility for future job options	Live in the right geographical locale	Move to a high future salary
Attorney for a public defender's office, handling criminal cases for indigent defendents	____	____	____	____
Attorney for a large law firm (20 or more attorneys) that specializes in corporate law	____	____	____	____
Attorney for a legal aid or legal services office, handling civil cases for poor persons	____	____	____	____
Attorney for a medium-sized law firm (10-16 attorneys) that specializes in business and corporate law	____	____	____	____
Attorney for a small law firm (2-6 attorneys) that does a large amount of free "public interest" law in addition to normal, income-producing work	____	____	____	____
Attorney for a small law firm (2-6 attorneys) with a general civil practice	____	____	____	____
Attorney for a non-profit "public interest" law center that specializes in environmental and consumer law	____	____	____	____
Attorney for an organization working to protect the rights of a racial minority group, such as the Native American Rights Fund or the NAACP	____	____	____	____

-9-

8 through 11 with a number from 1 to 5, using the following code:

5 = Much more likely to find attribute in this job type than in most other jobs
4 = Somewhat more likely to find attribute in this job type than in most other jobs
3 = About as likely to find attribute in this job type as in most other jobs
2 = Somewhat less likely to find attribute in this job type than in most other jobs
1 = Much less likely to find attribute in this job type than in most other jobs

Control your own work and work schedule	Gain experience, knowledge and contacts valuable to you	Feel the satisfaction of producing results	Receive guidance from experienced attorneys	Work in a congenial interpersonal atmosphere	Help persons/groups with whom you identify/sympathize
_____	_____	_____	_____	_____	_____
_____	_____	_____	_____	_____	_____
_____	_____	_____	_____	_____	_____
_____	_____	_____	_____	_____	_____
_____	_____	_____	_____	_____	_____
_____	_____	_____	_____	_____	_____
_____	_____	_____	_____	_____	_____
_____	_____	_____	_____	_____	_____

-10-

	Gain professional or community prestige	Do innovative and creative work	Have time to satisfy off-the-job interests	Work directly with clients
Attorney for a public defender's office, handling criminal cases for indigent defendants	____	____	____	____
Attorney for a large law firm (20 or more attorneys) that specializes in corporate law	____	____	____	____
Attorney for a legal aid or legal services office, handling civil cases for poor persons	____	____	____	____
Attorney for a medium-sized law firm (10-16 attorneys) that specializes in business and corporate law	____	____	____	____
Attorney for a small law firm (2-6 attorneys) that does a <u>large</u> amount of free "public interest" law in addition to normal, income-producing work	____	____	____	____
Attorney for a small law firm (2-6 attorneys) with a general civil practice	____	____	____	____
Attorney for a non-profit "public interest" law center that specializes in environmental and consumer law	____	____	____	____
Attorney for an organization working to protect the rights of a racial minority group, such as the Native American Rights Fund or the NAACP	____	____	____	____

-11-

Earn at least a moderate starting salary	Earn a high starting salary	Work for desired social and political goals	Have job security	Advance professionally with initial employer	Challenge your ability	Especially use your professional legal skills
____	____	____	____	____	____	____
____	____	____	____	____	____	____
____	____	____	____	____	____	____
____	____	____	____	____	____	____
____	____	____	____	____	____	____
____	____	____	____	____	____	____
____	____	____	____	____	____	____
____	____	____	____	____	____	____

29. Down the left-hand side of pages 12 and 14 are listed the 20 job types appearing before in this questionnaire. Across the top of pages 12 through 15, in abbreviated form, are listed eight of these same job types. In answering this question, you will make a series of comparisons between each of the jobs listed across the top of the page and each of the jobs listed down the side of the page. In each comparison you will state the minimum beginning yearly salary necessary to convince you to accept a job offer listed across the top for your initial job after graduating in preference to an offer for a job listed down the side of the page at the salary stated in parentheses. In other words, you are to state the lowest possible starting salary at which you would accept an offer for the option listed across the top in preference to an offer for the option listed down the side at the salary in parentheses. For example, in the first such comparison (denoted by an asterisk in the first blank space below), you are to state the lowest starting salary at which you would take a job for a large firm that specializes in corporate law (the second job listed across the top) in preference to a job with a public defender office at a starting salary of $15,000 (the first job listed down the side). You may state any salary, regardless of whether it reflects what a large firm would really pay, as long as it truly reflects the lowest starting salary at which you (continued at top of page 13)

	Public Defender Office	Large firm--corporate law	Legal Aid or Legal Services Office
Attorney for a public defender's office handling criminal cases for indigent defendants ($15,000)		* ________	________
Attorney for a large law firm (20 or more attorneys) that specializes in corporate law ($16,000)	________		________
Attorney for a legal aid or legal services office handling civil cases for poor persons ($13,000)	________	________	
Attorney for a medium-sized law firm (10-16 attorneys) that specializes in business and corporate law ($14,000)	________	________	________
Attorney for a small law firm (2-6 attorneys) that does a large amount of free "public interest" law in addition to normal, income-producing work ($10,000)	________	________	________
Attorney for a small firm (2-6 attorneys) with a general civil practice ($12,000)	________	________	________
Attorney for a non-profit "public interest" law center that specializes in environmental and consumer law ($12,000)	________	________	________
Attorney for an organization working to protect the rights of a racial minority group, such as the Native American Rights Fund or the NAACP ($15,000)	________	________	________

-13-

would choose that option. If, starting salary aside, you would prefer working for a large firm specializing in corporate law to working for a public defender, then the minimum you state should be less than $15,000--since you would probably be willing to sacrifice at least a few dollars to take the preferred job. How much less than $15,000 will depend upon the *degree to which*, starting salary aside, you would prefer working for a large firm. (Assume that the minimum you state for each job would also be paid to *all other* new law graduates taking that type of job, so that, compared to them, you would not be overpaid or underpaid.) If, starting salary aside, you would prefer working for a public defender office, then the minimum you state for taking the job with a large firm specializing in corporate law should be more than $15,000--to compensate you for doing the less preferred work. How much more than $15,000 will depend upon the *degree to which*, starting salary aside, you would prefer working for a public defender office. In every comparison, the same sort of reasoning should apply. If there is *absolutely no salary high enough* to persuade you to choose the option listed across the top, write "infinite" in the blank space. In each comparison, you are to assume that the two jobs in question constitute your only job offers and that your only additional option is unemployment for the foreseeable future. Each blank space denotes one comparison. First work from left to right across the top row. Then move down to the second row, and so on.

Medium-sized firm--business & corporate law	Small firm--much free public interest work	Small firm--general civil practice	Public interest law center--environmental & consumer law	Minority rights group--NAACP, NARF, etc.
______	______	______	______	______
______	______	______	______	______
______	______	______	______	______
	______	______	______	______
______		______	______	______
______	______		______	______
______	______	______		______
______	______	______	______	

-14-

	Public Defender Office	Large firm--corporate law	Legal Aid or Legal Services Office
Attorney for a small law firm (2-6 attorneys) that specializes in business law ($12,000)	______	______	______
Attorney for a small law firm (2-6 attorneys) that specializes in criminal and personal injury litigation ($11,000)	______	______	______
Attorney for a typical state or local governmental agency ($14,000)	______	______	______
Working for yourself as a solo practitioner, attempting to build a practice from whatever cases are available (estimated $8,000)	______	______	______
Clerk for a <u>state</u> supreme court justice ($15,000)	______	______	______
Attorney for a "public interest lobby" for which you did litigation, lobbying, investigative research, political organizing, and public relations ($13,000)	______	______	______
Deputy district attorney, prosecuting criminal cases ($13,000)	______	______	______
Attorney for a federal agency in the social services area, such as Health, Education and Welfare or Housing and Urban Development ($17,000)	______	______	______
House counsel for a large or medium-sized corporation ($16,000)	______	______	______
Attorney for a medium-sized law firm (10-16 attorneys) with a general civil practice ($14,000)	______	______	______
Staff attorney for the American Civil Liberties Union ($12,000)	______	______	______
Attorney for a federal regulatory agency such as the Securities and Exchange Commission or the Interstate Commerce Commission ($17,000)	______	______	______
No other firm offers yet, but not yet desperate (???????)	______	______	______

-15-

Medium-sized firm--business & corporate law	Small firm--much free public interest work	Small firm--general civil practice	Public interest law center--environmental & consumer law	Minority rights group--NAACP, NARF, etc.
________	________	________	________	________
________	________	________	________	________
________	________	________	________	________
________	________	________	________	________
________	________	________	________	________
________	________	________	________	________
________	________	________	________	________
________	________	________	________	________
________	________	________	________	________
________	________	________	________	________
________	________	________	________	________
________	________	________	________	________
________	________	________	________	________

ADDITIONAL INFORMATION RELATING TO QUESTION 29

Pretests indicate that it is very easy to become unkowingly confused and provide misleading information for Question 29. Please read the instructions to this question carefully and proceed with caution. When answering the question, it might help to refer back to the following summary of key points.

READ FULL INSTRUCTIONS TO QUESTION 29 BEFORE REFERRING TO THIS SUMMARY.

1. The minimum starting salary you write in each blank space should be the lowest possible starting salary at which you would accept an offer for the option listed across the top in preference to the option listed down the side at the starting salary stated in parentheses. Assume that these are your only two offers.

2. If, considering all factors other than starting salary, you prefer the option listed across the top to the option listed down the side, the figure you write in the blank space should be less than the salary in parentheses. How much less will depend upon the degree to which, starting salary aside, you prefer the option listed across the top.

3. If, considering all factors other than starting salary, you prefer the option listed down the side to the option listed across the top, the figure you write in the blank space should be more than the salary in parentheses. How much more will depend upon the degree to which, starting salary aside, you prefer the option listed down the side.

4. In order to avoid turning around instructions 2 and 3 above, it is important that you proceed with great care, referring to these instructions when necessary.

-16-

30. Can you think of any factors that will be extremely important in limiting your choice of jobs after graduating from law school? For example, are there personal factors that might limit your job choice to a particular geographical location or to limited working hours? Please describe any such factors.

31. In your opinion, what will be the minimum salary necessary for you to maintain a reasonable standard of living after graduating from law school?

32. Age: ___________

33. Sex: ___________

34. Race: 1.____Black 2.____Chicano 3.____Native American

4.____White 5.____Other (please identify ______________)

35. Marital status: 1.____Married 2.____Divorced or Widowed 3.____Single

36. Number of dependent children: ____________

37. Parents' primary occupations during your childhood:

Father: ______________________________

Mother: ______________________________

38. Undergraduate institution from which you graduated: __________________

39. Your score on the LSAT: ______________________________

40. Advanced degrees: ____________ ______________ __________________

degree discipline institution

41. If you pursued a career or some other activity after college and before starting law school, please briefly describe it.

Index

A Note on the Author

Robert V. Stover was an associate professor of political science at the University of Colorado, Boulder, Colorado. He received his Ph.D. from the University of Wisconsin, Madison, in 1972, and his J.D. from the University of Denver College of Law, Denver, Colorado, in 1980. His articles dealing with the U.S. legal system appeared in journals such as *Judicature, Law and Society Review,* and the *Justice Systems Journal*. He also co-authored several works with Don W. Brown which appeared in edited collections.

A Note on the Editor

Howard S. Erlanger is a professor in the law school and the department of sociology at the University of Wisconsin, Madison. He received his Ph.D. from the University of California at Berkeley and his J.D. from the University of Wisconsin Law School. His publications, which have appeared in such journals as the *American Sociological Review, Law and Society Review, Social Forces,* and the *American Bar Foundation Research Journal,* are primarily concerned with the sociology of the legal profession, focusing on socialization of law students, career patterns of public interest lawyers, and stratification in the profession.